Wendy Compson
and Margaret Lockley

First published 1981 by Floraprint Limited, Park Road, Calverton, Nottingham

© Floraprint Limited

ISBN 0 903001 46 2 (cased edition)

Editions Floraisse - Printed in France

Wendy Compson received her training in flower arranging at the Constance Spry Flower School in London. Having achieved her Diploma she gained further general experience by working in hotels, exhibitions and shops. Since then she has taught flower arrangement for local education authorities, schools and privately in her own flower school. She has written various articles for national and specialized magazines. Much of her spare time is at present spent in lecturing and demonstrating to women's clubs in East Anglia. Her energies are currently directed towards converting a field into a flower arranger's garden, following a move of house.

Wendy Compson (left) and Margaret Lockley

Margaret Lockley shares a love of plants with her husband Ralph, also a professional horticulturist. She began her career on the family's general nursery and then underwent training at Oaklands College of Agriculture and Horticulture, St. Albans and Swanley Women's College, Kent. She obtained her National Diploma in Horticulture, first in the General and later in the Commercial Vegetable Section and subsequently held posts in Warwickshire and Cambridgeshire. In recent years she has lectured and demonstrated on horticultural topics for the county council and Women's Institutes in Suffolk, where she now lives. She also contributes monthly gardening notes to the W.I. Federation newspaper.

Acknowledgments

The authors wish to thank Valerie Bone, Audrey Dalton, Mary Webb and Veronica and Patrick Rickards of Tuddenham Mill for their invaluable assistance in the preparation of this book.

Contents

PLANNING THE GARDEN

The garden storehouse
Everyone who has a garden, delights at some time to cut from the plants pieces for an indoor arrangement. It does not follow that cutting will spoil the overall outdoor effect. Careful choice of shrubs, herbaceous plants, herbs, bulbs and annuals will ensure a lovely garden with a succession of varied and fascinating material to cut from at every season of the year.

Hardiness
Some plants are hardy and able to withstand our climate without protection. Others need a little shade, shelter from wind, or a specially warm sunny corner. It is within the scope of most gardens to provide the right conditions for a wide variety of plants for cutting.

Soil types
Little need be said here about soil. The vast majority of plants will thrive on all but the heaviest clay or the thinnest chalky and sandy soils. Even these extremes can be modified by careful management and the addition of generous supplies of organic matter. Special requirements for individual plants are indicated in the subsequent chapters.

Shelter and aspects
It is wise to take stock first of the aspects existing in the garden. North, south, east and west facing, sunny, shady and windswept areas should be noted, for certain plants have preferences for shade, moisture, full sun or filtered sunlight. The next priority is to create a microclimate by providing shelter from wind so that as many species as possible can be encouraged to thrive.

Hedges, fences and shrub selection
Hedges, reed fencing, larch lap or other perimeter shelter will be needed, and after that a background of shrubs suitable for cutting and not so large, when full grown, as to be out of proportion to the size of the garden as a whole. The nurseryman will always advise about plant size and good catalogues give an indication by each species. Some evergreen and some deciduous species should be chosen. Evergreens come in a wide range of shapes, shades and sizes. Deciduous shrubs may be beautiful in flower, or at their best in autumn with gay fruit and foliage. Still others may provide fascinating shapes and colours in their bare winter twigs. There are many neat dwarf shrubs well suited to the smaller garden. Young shrubs should have space around them to allow for development and this, for the first few years, can be set with bulbs, herbs, annuals or herbaceous plants.

Vistas
It is satisfying to be able to see a particular group of plants from each window of the house; perhaps a summer border of herbaceous plants, a still group of water-loving species beside a pool, or a bed of plants with variegated foliage or contrasting leaf shapes. Other interesting features could include patio plants, container groups (freshly planted for each season) or a well-covered pergola. Use can be made of climbers to cover walls or scramble through trees and shrubs with surprising and delightful effects.

Paths
Paths from which plant material may be reached and cut are also necessary and can add greatly to the appearance of the whole garden design. Mowing stones alongside a lawn make a useful path in bad weather, while small random flagstones can break up the grass and save wear and tear in an area by which popular cutting material is growing. Bricks or cobbles set in design in patio areas can provide pockets of soil which make good homes for low growing dianthus, saxifrages, sedums and species of similar habit.

Special areas
If space permits and more annuals, biennials and herbaceous plants are needed than can be grown in the decorative garden, it is a good plan to reserve sunny areas behind the scenes to allow a cut flower garden to be developed when rows of helipterum, matthiola, saponaria or other favourite annuals or such perennials as *Scabiosa caucasica* can be grown in effective quantities.

The flower arranger can then have the best of both worlds – attractive borders and almost unlimited material for cutting.

These areas, if carefully planned, can provide a useful link in rotation with the vegetable garden crops.

The scope of this book
Our selection of plants is designed to provide large and small gardens with varied material for use and colour at each season of the year.

The chapter with detailed notes on planting, pruning and propagation should be used in conjunction with the notes given under each genus. Similarly the chapter on arranging augments notes on containers, arrangements and material preparation given under the genera.

A grey and silver collection for a patio or island bed needs an open, sunny aspect. It would make an interesting feature for all seasons. It would fill in within three years and a reserve of young plants should be rooted in a cold frame for spring replacements.

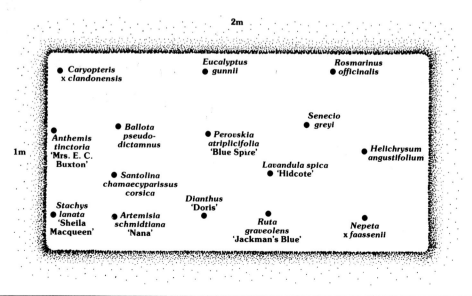

FLOWER ARRANGING

Flower arranging is one of those interests that needs very little capital outlay initially. You may be saying to yourself, 'What about the cost of flowers?' Well, the whole object of this book is to help you select suitable plants to grow that will provide you with arranging material throughout the year, thereby keeping your costs to a minimum.

Care and handling of flowers

When a flower is picked from a plant, it is obvious that one's objective should be to keep it as fresh as possible for as long as possible. When a flower or stem is severed from a plant its natural food and water sources are removed. If cut at the correct stage of growth the stem will need only water to last almost as long as in its natural state, provided the material has been correctly conditioned and hardened.

If possible, all cut flowers and foliage should be stood in deep water in a cool, dark place for some hours, or preferably overnight, before use. All flowers and foliage, unless freshly cut, should have about 1.25 cm cut from the stem ends before being put in water and the lower leaves should be removed; this is particularly important with soft flowers such as stock, marigolds, asters etc., whose leaves quickly decompose in water.

Hard wooded flowers and foliage should be recut at the end and then hammered or split, as this enables the water to travel more easily up the stem. Always cut stems on a slant, because this gives twice as much surface area through which water can be absorbed. If the stems must be hammered, do so with a mallet, on a block of wood. (The bark can be scraped off first, exposing the white wood.) Transpiration is the giving-off of moisture through the stomata or pores. It is at its height in a hot, dry atmosphere, therefore plant material is put in a cool, dark place in deep water to reduce the rate of transpiration as much as possible and also to retard the development of the blooms.

Drying and preserving of material
There are several methods of drying and preserving but the ones I have mostly referred to are:
  1. Doing what comes naturally.
  2. Hanging.
  3. Glycerining.
  4. Desiccants.

Doing what comes naturally
Some plant forms of good colour, texture and shape dry out and preserve themselves in a pleasing manner all on their own out in the garden, by a pool or by the roadside. They should be picked at perfection in dry weather and stored in boxes of suitable sizes.

Hanging
Keep bunches small and hang the material upside down preferably in the airing cupboard for a few days. In the kitchen there is too big a risk of steam. The ideal room is somewhere dark and airy although airiness is not so vital as long as the bunches are kept small and the conditions are conducive to speedy drying. Immediately after drying take down bunches and store carefully in boxes or clear plastic bags.

Glycerining
A solution will have to be made up from one part glycerine to two parts boiling water which is essential to facilitate the intake of the solution. Stir the mixture well and use it hot. Any left over mixture may be used again even if it is discoloured but reboil and use it hot. As with all material, gather when stems are full of sap

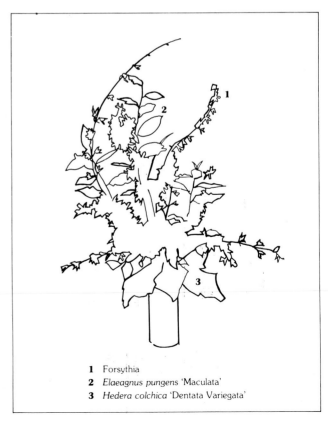

1 Forsythia
2 Elaeagnus pungens 'Maculata'
3 Hedera colchica 'Dentata Variegata'

and pick off any damaged leaves. After gathering material, recut and leave in water for twenty-four hours or overnight, then put in glycerine solution to a depth of 5 cm up the stem. The length of time you leave the material varies but if you turn the leaves over it will be possible to see quite clearly the glycerine entering the veins and this should be a good guide to the right time to remove the material from the solution. If material is left too long in the solution the leaves will become sticky and go mouldy.

To get a lovely variation in colours after glycerining put the leaves in a dry jar and place in direct sunlight. This will bleach them to golden shades of various hues. For a dark colour leave some pieces in the dark.

Desiccants

This method entails rapid drying with the aid of drying agents. Substances such as borax, alum, silver sand, silica gel or one of the named products on the market can be used. These substances take moisture speedily from the material drawing it into themselves, whilst the colour and contours of the plant material are left intact.

You will require a deep plastic or tin box with a tight fitting lid. Put a 3 cm deep layer of desiccant in the box, place your flowers in the substance and then gently cover them up completely using a teaspoon to spoon the desiccant between the petals. Seal the container and place it in a warm, dry place for two to three days or two to three weeks depending on the flower, amount of heat and desiccant chosen. Store the dried flowers where it is warm and where there is good air circulation away from strong light.

Equipment

Tools

The equipment you require can be collected over a number of years but I will go over the items you need. Probably the most important tool of the trade is something for cutting. Secateurs are ideal for gathering your material from the garden and for the preparation of woody stems, but it is a good idea to invest in a good quality pair of flower scissors. The best kind have one straight edge for stem cutting, a serrated edge for cutting wire netting or stub wires and a little notch where the blades join for cutting the thicker stems. Never cut wires with secateurs, it will render them totally useless. Also, do not be tempted by cheap, imported flower scissors; they may seem a good buy at the time, but you are lucky if they last one season.

Other items that I find desirable additions to the flower arranger's cupboard are a really good dust-sheet, if possible made of PVC with handles either at the sides or on all four corners. A watering can with a very long spout is excellent for topping up. A mister is useful for spraying finished arrangements, particularly those that you cannot water too often such as flower festival pieces.

Containers

Containers for your flowers are items to be collected over a period of time. Gone are the days when you could go into an antique shop and ask to look in their oddments box and find wonderful pieces of china, glass, copper and brass which were literally going for a few pence. What treasure troves those boxes were. Nowadays we have to rely on friends and relations turning cupboards out to find the unusual container. Potters are now much more aware of the need to produce pots and dishes suitable for flowers. Some companies do produce china vases in various shapes and sizes for the arranger, so it is a case of collecting containers as and when you can.

Flower holders

Once you have some vases the next item to think about is what to put inside them to keep the flowers in place. You really have a choice of three things, Oasis, wire netting and pin holder. When I teach my students I always insist they use wire netting in my classes for two reasons; the first is that it is the cheapest method and the second is that once you can arrange satisfactorily in wire netting you can arrange flowers in all sorts of shaped vases.

The secret of wire netting is to use the 5 cm mesh and crumple it up so that you have all shapes and sizes of holes, pushing the netting well down into the container and leaving at least 2·5 cm above the top of the container.

Oasis must be really well soaked, preferably overnight in a plastic box filled with water and the lid tightly closed to keep the block under the water. It can then be cut into any shape you like with a sharp knife.

Pinholders can be used when arranging a few flowers on a plate or shallow dish. They should be stuck to the container with a little piece of Oasis-fix which is similar to plasticine but far more bonding. Try to ensure that the base of the pinholder and the container are dry before sticking the Oasis-fix to them.

Basic shapes for arrangements

Facing arrangement

When practising this arrangement, I suggest you use a

bread baking tin. Use 5 cm wire netting mesh, a piece about six times the size of the top of the container; stretch the piece out and then fold in the corners and roll it like a parcel. Push the wire right down, making five to seven layers, with about 2·5 cm protruding out of the container. If the container has a rim, cut the netting to hook just under the rim in about four places. Fill the container about three-quarters full. Start the arrangement about three-quarters of the way back; it is not necessary to push the stems right down. Make the outline first, then the stems must radiate from the centre of the arrangement. It is essential to have a good rough background to begin with. When the outline is completed with the foliage then you can use the flowers, tilting them slightly backwards. Place an upright piece of foliage in the centre to start with, this will be your highest point, then sketch your outline in as if you were making a fan shape remembering to bring the two side pieces well over the edges.

Think about your composition carefully, avoiding separate groups of colour because the result will be patchy. Do not use too many flowers of the same

length. When you have finished tidy up the back with a little foliage, remembering to trim leaves and foliage so that there are no leaves below the water line. Top up the container when you have finished the arrangement.

An all-round bowl
Make the wire netting into five or six layers, and it can be attached with silver wire, rather like a parcel, or use a round, soaked Oasis in a dish or container. Start with a reasonably pointed piece of foliage for the centre stripping off its lower leaves. This piece of foliage must be standing upright in the centre, not too large with all the flowers and foliage radiating from this point of the vase. Then put in four pieces of foliage of equal length at the quarter hours of the clock, take four more shorter pieces and place them in between the quarter hours. Before you place any flowers in the arrangement add about eight more smaller pieces of foliage between the centre piece and the stems at the base. Do not work in sections or completely on one side, but the flowers must be in groups, not too many of the same length; the flowers round the edge must lie down. The arrangement is almost of pyramid shape. As you are working, turn the bowl round all the time working from side to side, remembering to put in one or two short pieces to give some depth.

A table centre
This arrangement can be practised in an oblong baking tin with wire netting. Place a piece of foliage at either end long and low, and two shorter pieces out at the sides, the centre piece must also be low. Gradually build up to a pointed flower in the centre keeping the larger flowers in the centre. There should be no two stems the same length on the sides, and the corners must not be too square. All the flowers go up to the centre.

A dish or plate arrangement
This arrangement is one that uses a pinholder secured to the container when both surfaces are dry using Oasis-fix. Start off using about five pieces of foliage graduating downwards in height then do the same with five or seven flowers and finally use some large leaves such as bergenia or hosta at the base to help conceal the pinholder.

Moss gardens on wooden slabs
When the small spring bulbs come out it is rather pretty to arrange them in little jars on a wooden slab. I conceal the jars with moss and if I want varying heights I put pieces of Oasis on the slab and then put the jars on the Oasis.

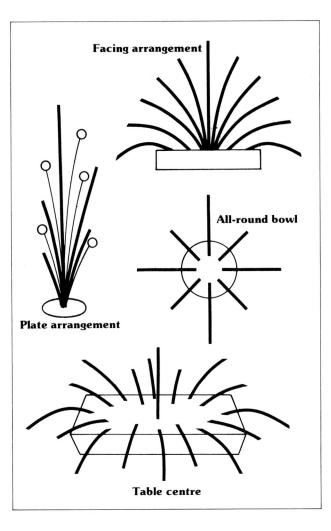

Facing arrangement

Plate arrangement

All-round bowl

Table centre

CULTURAL HINTS

General preparation for planting

Careful preparation for planting, whether shrubs or smaller plants, will always reward the gardener in later years. Land must be clean of perennial weeds and in as friable a condition as possible, neither bone-dry, waterlogged, nor frozen.

Certain weedkillers may be used for persistent weeds, or land may be fallowed for the first season so that weed growth can be forked out.

Include well rotted compost, leaf-mould or damp peat and a light dusting of bonemeal in all soil which is to receive new plants. Most decorative plants are happy in a neutral or slightly acid soil so lime need not be added. Lime-loving plants and those tolerant of alkaline conditions are indicated in the individual lists. Have your garden plan prepared and undertake a little planting at a time, starting with those plants intended to be main features. The use of container grown stock has made it possible to introduce new plants at almost any time of year, but lifted nursery stock is still bought and quite often gardeners raise cuttings which they wish to transplant. In these cases there is an optimum time for planting. Evergreens seem generally to transplant most happily in early autumn or late spring. Deciduous shrubs will transplant well between October and March.

Planting shrubs and conifers

When taking out earth for shrubs or conifers, make quite sure each hole is wide enough for the roots and deep enough for the plant to be set to the original nursery level usually recognized by a soil line on the stem. Lower soil is usually paler than top soil; add the organic matter to the lower soil, mixing it with some of the extracted top soil. This will provide a kindly rooting medium for the new plant. Mound the base soil a little.

Use sharp secateurs to trim off any damaged roots and with container grown plants, gently tease the roots out a little and loosen the root ball slightly to encourage roots to extend into the fresh, surrounding earth in the hole. Never let any root turn upward. In dry periods, add water before replacing the remaining soil round the roots.

Firm the soil little by little, heel to the outer edge of the hole, toe slightly pointing upward toward the bush. Lift and shake the plant gently to settle the soil as you fill in.

Where stakes are used, treat the lower half before-

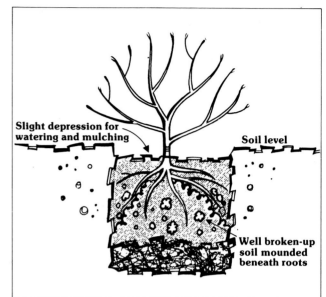

Planting a bare root shrub

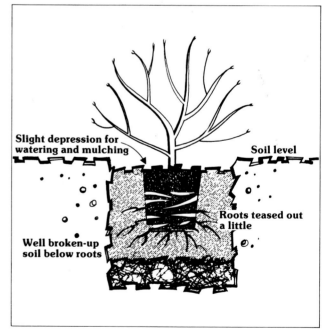

Planting a container grown shrub

hand, with a fungicide. Good adjustable tree ties may be purchased to prevent stakes chafing the stems and these can be altered as the stem girth increases. Plastic rabbit guards are also available for susceptible plants.

If a slight depression is left round each plant, this can usefully be filled with water during dry spells. A mulch of well rotted compost on the surface, as well as below the roots, helps to retain water in the soil and to keep the plant alive.

A special spray for reducing transpiration on evergreens during replanting is useful and may save many specimens if drought occurs during the first season after planting.

To begin with, shrubs grow more freely if not surrounded and choked by grass. As they become established, the area may be grassed down, if wished.

Planting herbaceous perennials

Plants in this group need an unmounded bed of soil, 10 cm below the level of surrounding lawn or pathway. This not only retains moisture for the plants but allows for mulching and deters birds from scattering soil on surrounding areas.

Many of the fibrous rooted types of herbaceous perennials are remarkably shallow rooted and only ask to be quickly tucked into the top soil before the roots dry out. Buds should be just showing at ground level. In many cases, groups of three or five plants are more effective than single specimens.

The fleshy rooted types need deeper holes to take the full root depth and again must not be allowed to dry out, so keep the roots to be planted in between layers of damp sacking. In cases where existing clumps are being divided, aim to keep the young outer growths and discard the woody centre. Autumn or early spring are the best transplanting times. For primroses or pyrethrum division is best as soon as the flowers fade.

Planting bulbs and corms

As a general guide, these plants need to be their own depth below ground level, that is an 8 cm bulb needs to have its base 16 cm below ground level. As seasons pass, bulbs will themselves usually adjust to individual ideal depths and top dressings of rotted leaf-mould or compost after foliage has died down, will ensure that they remain well covered. Most bulbs and corms increase naturally, depending on soil type and the presence or absence of slugs and mice. All appreciate a liquid feed after flowering.

Most are planted in autumn, using a trowel. Gladioli, which are not quite hardy, are best planted in spring and lifted each autumn.

Sowing annuals and biennials

On the whole, annuals prefer sunny sites. Although the soil need not be rich, the better it is prepared, the better the annuals will grow and the longer will be their flowering period. Many hardy kinds, such as calendula and clarkia can be sown direct as long as the seed bed is fine and firm. The bed may need protection with twigs and black cotton as birds often fancy a dust bath just after seed has been sown.

If the bed is devoted to annuals, the different seeds may be sown in parallel short drills or in patches of soil. Drills can be drawn very shallow with the point of a label and the seed covered to just its own depth. Where patches are sown, score across the area both ways with a label and again sow in the score marks, lightly levelling afterwards with the back of a rake.

Half hardy annuals, such as nemesia and zinnia raised indoors, need hardening off. For this purpose and many others, a cold frame is a very good investment in any garden, with or without a greenhouse.

Thin direct sown annuals (thinnings may often be transplanted) and to maintain flower supplies, keep the dead flowers cut off.

Small twigs among the young plants will provide inconspicuous support as the stems grow.

Such biennial plants as myosotis and cheiranthus are sown one year to flower the next. Sowing time is usually in May or June, and seed is sown in a seed bed, the little plants being transplanted to a nursery bed and from there, in autumn, to final flowering positions. On the whole, they too prefer sunny, open sites although myosotis grows happily from seed sown in filtered shade. At final planting, cheiranthus particularly benefits from a light dusting of sulphate of potash over the flowering site.

The spacing of annual and biennial plants will often make a vast difference to their habit of growth. Crowded, unthinned seedlings tend to grow tall, thin and almost unbranched. Those which are widely spaced will usually develop into bushy, free flowering plants providing main and side shoots for the arranger. Cultivation methods must be followed which produce the kind of plant required to suit the floral art in question.

Cutting plant material for arranging

It is a sad reflection on the public at large that every year *Salix caprea,* the pussy willow and *Ilex aquifolium,* the holly are vandalised by thoughtless, tearing hands to such an extent that bushes seldom recover their natural graceful habit.

Flower arrangers have a reputation for cutting plants indiscriminately. This is a pity and need not be perpetuated if, before gathering material, they pose this question, 'Am I cutting correctly or spoiling the ultimate shape of my plant?'

In days gone by, the private gardener, with his feeling for and love of the plants he tended, would cut the flowers for the house leaving plant shapes unimpaired.

With a little more thought and guidance, today's flower arranger could do this too. Here are a few basic guidelines to help keep plants in good form.

General note on time of cutting
Choose cool, still weather, in early morning or late evening when stems are full of sap. Avoid cutting in high wind or in the heat of the day when everything growing is limp and almost flagging.

Shrubs and trees
By standing back and making a careful survey of a well grown plant, it will be easy to see the inconspicuous places from which strong, woody material may be cut without spoiling the balance of the whole. These places may be:
  a. at the back of or inside the bush,
  b. where one branch crosses or is rubbing on another, or
  c. where one branch lies closely above and parallel to another.
With so wide a choice, it is never necessary to snip from the front of a bush.

Having decided on the best branch to cut, use sharp secateurs and cut low down, just above a joint. Never mind if the branch is longer than needed: keep the surplus in a cool place for a future arrangement. Properly prepared, this woody material will not need to be renewed every few days but will serve over a long period in several consecutive arrangements. This applies particularly to branches cut in winter and to evergreen material.

Next in importance is the point at which to cut. As in normal pruning, cuts should always be made to a joint, that is a leaf, bud or joint should be at the top of the wood left on the branch when cut material has been removed.

The buds which will develop from this joint will keep the wood alive and prevent any rot setting in. Where a snag is left without a joint, rot almost invariably follows and this decay may spread down the bush stem. A snag is the long piece of twig left above a living bud when a pruning cut is made too high. Having no bud at its tip, the snag is almost certain to die back at least to the top live bud and often further down the stem.

It may be appropriate to indicate here the usual patterns of bud formation commonly found in shrubs and trees. Some, such as syringa (lilac) and forsythia, have buds in opposite pairs. Others, such as rosa and spiraea have buds arranged spirally on the twigs. Corylus (hazel) and magnolia buds grow alternately in slightly zig-zag fashion.

A bud develops in the axil of each leaf stem (that is

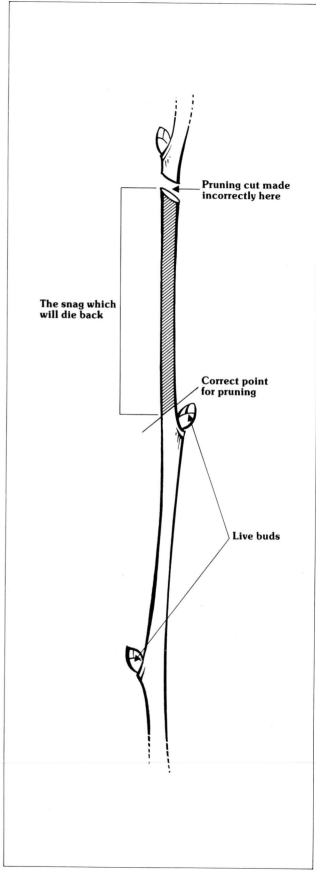

Pruning cut made incorrectly here

The snag which will die back

Correct point for pruning

Live buds

A pruning snag

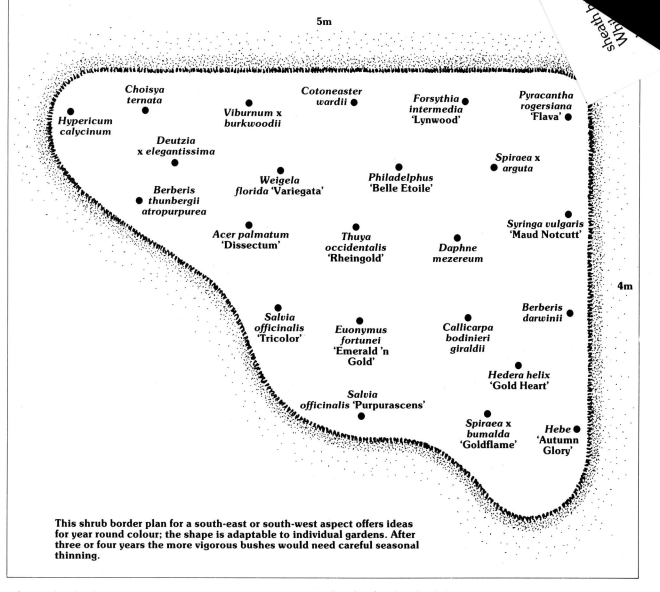

5m

Choisya
ternata

Cotoneaster
wardii

Forsythia
intermedia
'Lynwood'

Pyracantha
rogersiana
'Flava'

Hypericum
calycinum

Viburnum x
burkwoodii

Deutzia
x elegantissima

Spiraea x
arguta

Weigela
florida 'Variegata'

Philadelphus
'Belle Etoile'

Berberis
thunbergii
atropurpurea

Syringa vulgaris
'Maud Notcutt'

Acer palmatum
'Dissectum'

Thuya
occidentalis
'Rheingold'

Daphne
mezereum

4m

Salvia
officinalis
'Tricolor'

Euonymus
fortunei
'Emerald 'n
Gold'

Callicarpa
bodinieri
giraldii

Berberis
darwinii

Hedera helix
'Gold Heart'

Salvia
officinalis 'Purpurascens'

Spiraea x
bumalda
'Goldflame'

Hebe
'Autumn
Glory'

This shrub border plan for a south-east or south-west aspect offers ideas
for year round colour; the shape is adaptable to individual gardens. After
three or four years the more vigorous bushes would need careful seasonal
thinning.

where the leaf stem joins the twig). From a careful study of leaf and bud arrangement at the joints, it becomes easier to recognise the right places (from the plant's point of view) to cut branches, whether in routine pruning or for flower arranging.

A bud normally grows into a new shoot following the direction in which the bud originally pointed and it is with this in mind that the joint or the place for cutting should be selected.

Herbaceous perennials

When cutting material for arrangements, use sharp secateurs or a really sharp bladed knife or good garden scissors. Never pull, bend or snap stems, always cut cleanly, just above a joint leaving some live, green leaves behind to continue growing on the plant.

In decorative borders, either select stems from the back of individual clumps or cut to thin and space out the remaining flower stems. Never hack the whole of the material required from one clump.

Cut when flowers are dry. Evening, before the dew falls, is often the best time.

Unless seed heads are wanted for dried decoration, always cut faded heads off herbaceous plants in good time. Quite often a few weeks later a small second crop of flowers will develop. In the colder areas, the lower part of woody stems can be left on herbaceous clumps until growth begins in spring. It makes useful frost protection.

Bulbs and corms

Always cut the stems, never pull them from the ground and if foliage is needed, select from a wide area rather than spoil one group by excessive cutting. Narcissi of all kinds last longest if cut when the bud

...as just burst.

...e beautiful in flower, bulbs and corms are rather unsightly when only the leaves remain. One should resist the temptation to tidy them up as the leaves are the only means by which new underground food stores can be nourished for the following year. So cut off dead flower heads by all means, and give a liquid feed. Then allow the foliage to die down undisturbed. This pinpoints the advantage of growing these genera in grass, naturalising where the grass can be left unmown until mid-summer. They may equally well be grown among shrubs where the leaves do not look out of place.

Routine pruning

For routine pruning, there are fairly simple rules for the seasonal groups. Many shrubs need no regular pruning at all, and special requirements are indicated in the list of individual genera which follows these general chapters.

Group one includes plants grown specially for winter stem colour, such as *Cornus alba* 'Sibirica' and plants which flower in late summer on wood made during that season, such as *Buddleia davidii* and *Caryopteris* x *clandonensis*.

This group is pruned in February or March, cutting previous year's wood back to fairly low buds.

Group two includes shrubs which flower in early spring on wood made the previous year, such as *Jasminum nudiflorum* and *Forsythia* x *intermedia*.

In order to encourage fresh wood to grow and flower the following year, some older wood should be cut out each spring soon after the flowers are over.

Group three includes shrubs flowering in early summer on wood made the previous year, such as philadelphus and weigela.

The principle is the same as in Group two: removal of older wood and encouragement of new stems to keep the bush within bounds and the flowers within reach. Carry out the pruning as soon as the flowers fade.

Group four mainly concerns evergreens and little grey foliage shrubs, such as rosmarinus, santolina, *Senecio greyi,* olearia and hebe.

Evergreens which have been frost or wind damaged during winter, will often break afresh from just above ground level if hard pruned in April, just as new growth begins. Santolina keeps its neat bushy outline if pruned this way each year. Other evergreens such as buxus, ilex and arbutus, which have formal shapes, need straggly shoots pruned back with secateurs at this same season.

Propagation

Amateurs are often enthusiastic to try to grow new plants themselves by seed or by vegetative means. The methods suggested in this book are those most suited to the amateur with fairly limited facilities.

The term indoors indicates a warm kitchen window-sill or a heated greenhouse. A cold frame can be any protected wooden or brick structure with a glass or clear plastic cover. It need not, for the purpose of this book be in full sunlight. It will provide shelter for germinating seeds, small seedlings which may not be fully hardy, and for half ripened wood cuttings for their first eight months.

A propagating frame, box or case is a small enclosed structure within a warm kitchen or greenhouse. Being covered with glass or plastic it is even warmer and more humid than the surrounding air. Seeds will germinate quickly and soft wood cuttings should root readily in these conditions. They do not need to remain in the frame very long but should be moved to gradually cooler conditions as soon as growth has begun.

There are three types of cutting, soft, half ripened and hard wood. Soft cuttings are immature stems needing warm protection until rooted. Half ripened cuttings are those shoots which are half way through their growing season, needing cool protection while rooting and until the following spring. Hard wood cuttings are taken in autumn from ripened young wood and are generally stout enough to be rooted out of doors.

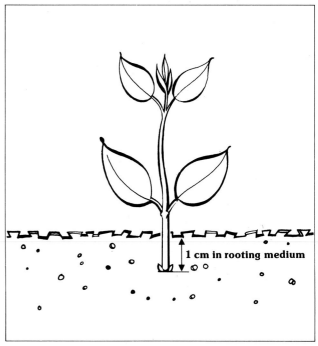

1 cm in rooting medium

Soft cutting

Budding and grafting more often than not are in the field of the expert.

Stratified seeds are those inside berries which are layered (i.e. in strata) with sand or soil in a pot, which is plunged to its rim outdoors over winter. As the berry flesh rots away, the seeds mature and will begin to grow either the first or second spring. The little plants can be transplanted the following autumn.

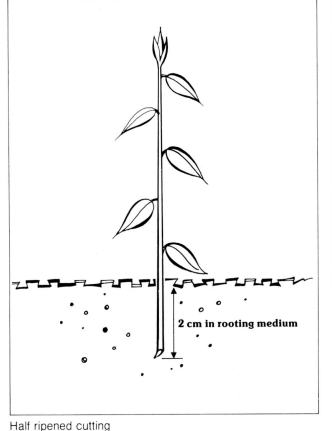

2 cm in rooting medium

Half ripened cutting

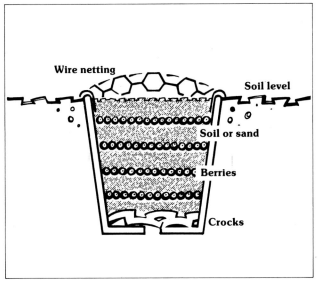

Wire netting

Soil level

Soil or sand

Berries

Crocks

Stratified seed

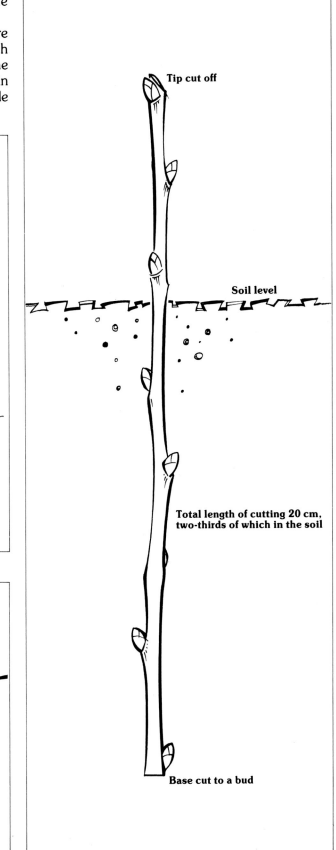

Tip cut off

Soil level

Total length of cutting 20 cm, two-thirds of which in the soil

Base cut to a bud

Hardwood cutting

15

AN A~Z OF GARDEN PLANTS
TO GROW AND CUT FOR ARRANGING

The Royal Horticultural Society established a hallmark for good garden plants when it created the Award of Garden Merit (AGM) as an acknowledgment that expert plantsmen from the RHS considered species so labelled worthy of inclusion in the garden. The heights given beside each species are only an approximate guide to mature size. Growth of individual plants depends so much on soil type, area, temperature, aspect and rainfall that nothing more specific has been attempted.

Acanthus mollis

Acanthus

mollis	1 – 1·3 m
spinosus AGM	70 cm – 1m

These are herbaceous perennials for the back of a border or they may be grown as specimen plants in partial shade when the full beauty of the glossy foliage is seen to advantage.
They come from southern Europe and North Africa and both grow happily in any good loam.
They seed quite freely and roots may also be divided in early spring.

Arranging
These are very valuable plants with ornamental foliage sometimes providing shiny green leaves up to 60 cm long which are most useful at the base of large arrangements. The long stems bearing white and purple flowers add height to mixed summer vases of blues, mauves and pinks.

Preparation
Pick only when all the flowers are open and then dip stem ends in boiling water and follow with a long cold drink. The cut leaf ends should be dipped in boiling water and then in a weak starch solution which is made up by dissolving two teaspoonfuls of instant starch in 0·85 litres of water. Leave material in the solution overnight to stiffen slightly. Dry by hanging method.

Acer

palmatum 'Atropurpureum'	3 – 6 m
palmatum 'Dissectum'	1 – 3 m
pseudoplatanus 'Brilliantissimum'	3 m

These maples, all deciduous, like a well-drained loam and *A. palmatum* varieties welcome light shade from taller bushes during the hottest of our summer days. They are among the most dependable shrubs for brilliant coloured foliage, *A.p.* 'Brilliantissimum' particularly in spring, the palmatum varieties in spring and again in autumn. *A.p.* 'Atropurpureum' is bronzy throughout the summer.

None of the three kinds makes rampant growth and in our drier areas all are distinctly slow growing. They need no regular pruning: dead branches, or any exceeding their allotted space, may be cut out.

When bought in containers, by far the best method as they resent root disturbance, make sure the roots are gently loosened in the ball to encourage them to develop into the new earth provided at the planting site.

Seed of *A. palmatum* is sometimes available. This should be sown outdoors in spring. Usually the three varieties listed here are grafted onto rootstocks.

Arranging

These shrubs are wonderful for autumn colour and complement the many berries available in September and October. *A.p.* 'Brilliantissimum' has a most unusual foliage in the spring when the peach tinted leaves are quite beautiful arranged with a few similarly coloured tulips.

Preparation

Stems should be hammered and placed in deep warm water. Individual leaves can be pressed.

Achillea filipendulina 'Coronation Gold'

Acer palmatum 'Dissectum'

Achillea

filipendulina 'Coronation Gold'	90 cm
filipendulina 'Gold Plate' AGM	1·5 m
millefolium 'Lilac Beauty'	75 cm
ptarmica 'The Pearl'	75 cm
serrata 'W.B. Child'	75 cm
taygetea	60 cm

This happy herbaceous genus, with species coming from many parts of the world, will grow in almost any soil and flowers best in open, sunny borders.

'The Pearl', of rather different habit from the rest and with white flowers, grows well in semi-shade and needs staking if long, straight stems are required. Other varieties have stout stems and flattish heads of small flowers.

'W.B. Child', white, starts to flower in May, followed by the others from July until the autumn. If cutting is begun early, the taller varieties remain a little more compact than the heights above suggest.

A. taygetea, which has grey foliage and lemon-yellow flower heads is less rampant than the others.

They divide easily in early spring and to maintain quality, should be replanted every two or three years into freshly prepared soil.

Arranging

My favourite way of using achillea is to put three or

five pieces in a pinholder on a black plate coming down in height and alternating with pieces of *Echinops ritro*. The contrast in shape gives a lovely effect.

Preparation
These long lasting flowers just need a diagonal cut. They preserve well by the hanging method.

Agapanthus 'Headbourne Hybrids'

Agapanthus

campanulatus 'Albus'		75 cm
campanulatus 'Isis'		75 cm
'Headbourne Hybrids'	AGM	70 – 90 cm

African lilies, with their clustered heads of blue or white flowers are ideal for growing in tubs or containers which can be moved to a frost-free shelter during the winter. However, in many areas, on well drained sheltered borders, the plants will survive our winters outdoors if light litter of straw or bracken, is spread over the surface in autumn.
The 'Headbourne Hybrids' are hardier than other species.
Plants raised from seed begin to flower in three or four years, gaining size as the years pass. Established clumps and hybrids may be divided in March, but the crowns do not enjoy disturbance, preferring to be top dressed with well rotted organic matter each spring and left to increase naturally for a number of years. During the growing season, ample moisture is necessary to produce good flower stems.
Cut off dead heads as the blooms fade unless these are to be kept for decoration.

Arranging
The 'Headbourne Hybrids' and 'Isis' varieties add a touch of blue to a late summer arrangement, but do not forget that blue is absorbed when seen from a distance, so leave them out of church pedestals.

Preparation
Diagonal cut and a good drink. Dry by hanging up the mature seed heads.

Alchemilla

mollis AGM	30 cm

Any shaded or part shaded moist soil will suit this dainty perennial with long lasting flower heads and silky, lobed leaves.

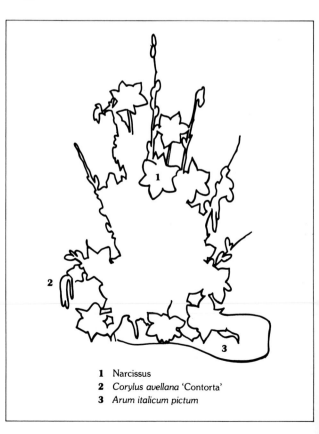

1 Narcissus
2 *Corylus avellana* 'Contorta'
3 *Arum italicum pictum*

It will often produce seedlings in the vicinity and is generally better from seed than from division.

Arranging
I think this is probably my favourite plant, particularly with the early morning dew making fairytale cobwebs over the leaves. The flowering spikes add an unusual lime green dimension to vases of greens and yellows. It is such a light material that it will give a showering effect. The foliage consisting of soft green leaves forms an excellent backdrop for so many summer flowers including roses.

Preparation
A diagonal cut and a good long drink with lower leaves removed. Dry by hanging after removing foliage.

Alchemilla mollis

Allium

aflatunense	1 m
christophii (albopilosum)	50 cm
giganteum	1·2 m
karataviense	15 cm
ostrowskianum	30 cm
schubertii	30 cm
siculum	90 cm
sphaerocephalum	50 cm
tuberosum	45 cm

With the bulbs of these unusual plants so reasonably priced, it is surprising that they are not more widely planted. Although related to the onion, unless the leaves are bruised the characteristic odour is not noticeable.

All these fascinating species thrive in sunny, open sites, preferably on light soil. The smaller species are happy on the rock garden while *A. giganteum,* deep lilac, is at home in a woodland setting. They are long lasting blooms in a wide range of colours from red and pink to purple, blue and white. Even the leaves of *A. karataviense,* pink, are mottled. Seed heads are durable too. The long flowering season extends from May until October, *A. tuberosum,* white, being the last to flower.

They may be raised from seed sown in spring in a cold frame or from offsets detached after the bulbs have flowered.

Arranging
These plants provide long lasting cut material in a variety of colours which can always find a place in any number of arrangements. The large flowers look very good when used in a pedestal arrangement, taking away any flatness produced by using too many similar shaped materials.

Preparation
A diagonal cut. For drying, cut in full bloom and hang.

Allium karataviense

Alstroemeria 'Ligtu Hybrids'

Alstroemeria

aurantiaca	70 cm
'Ligtu Hybrids'	50 cm – 1 m

If planted in deep soil on sheltered, well drained borders, protected with bracken or peat in winter, these beautiful Peruvian lilies should prove to be hardy, although *A. aurantiaca* is rather more hardy than the 'Ligtu Hybrids'.

The fleshy root tubers need planting 15 cm deep to start with. In heavy soil, mix sharp sand with the soil at planting time. With the 'Ligtu Hybrids', it is best to start with pot-grown tubers and too many flowers must not be expected during the first season.

New beds should be left undisturbed for a number of years, until flower size decreases, when the roots may be divided and replanted on a fresh site in April. Once established, the tubers go to unusual depths and plants may be found growing on the site of an earlier bed in after years.

Seed may be sown as soon as ripe, in pots in a cold frame, growing the seedlings on without disturbance until the second year, and then planting out direct from pots 20 – 30 cm apart. Seedlings take several years to reach flowering stage.

If a cool greenhouse is available, the 'Ligtu Hybrids' may be grown in pots of light, rich compost with generous water in summer and very little in winter.

Arranging

These multi-headed flower stems with their delicate pastel shades can be used either in big arrangements as they grow, or pieces can be taken off the heads and used individually. From one large head broken down I managed to make a delightful show in a candle cup with a matching candle and some feathery foliage. It was a charming dinner party centre piece using very little material.

Preparation

A diagonal cut, or if stems are very tough, split and hammer gently. Seed heads can be dried by hanging.

Amaranthus caudatus

Amaranthus

caudatus   50 – 60 cm
caudatus 'Viridis'   50 – 60 cm

Half hardy annuals from India, these unusual plants need careful raising from seed sown indoors in spring. Hardening off must be gradual and outdoor temperatures quite warm before final planting out is done. They both prefer sunny sites and good soil. The closer they are set and the poorer the soil, the smaller will be the ultimate flower tassels.

If seed is sown direct outdoors, delay until the soil is really warm and thin early after germination.

Arranging

These trailing tassels of red or green are best used after removing the leaves. A wonderful asset to the arranger who needs material to cascade over the edge of the container, the green variety gives a cool effect when used with other rich colours.

Preparation

Remove all leaves and place stem ends in very hot water. Leave for a good long drink. Dry by hanging.

Amelanchier

lamarckii (canadensis)   6 – 8 m

Amelanchier, the snowy mespilus, comes from North America and is such a delightful shrub in spring and autumn that it merits a good open site, preferably against a dark background when the changing colours of spring shoots, scattered racemes of white blossoms and rich autumn foliage tints can be fully appreciated.

Regular pruning is not needed but straggling shoots may be cut back after flowering.

It may be raised from seed sown in spring or from layers in spring. It is not easy from cuttings.

Arranging

This shrub is used mainly for its beautiful autumnal shades of reds and yellows which blend with flowers of similar colour, such as dahlias, in the autumn.

Preparation

Split and hammer stem ends, then give a good drink.

Amelanchier lamarckii (canadensis)

Anaphalis triplinervis

Anaphalis

margaritacea	50 cm
triplinervis AGM	30 cm
yedoensis	70 cm

These good-natured grey-leafed perennials, sometimes known as immortelle or pearly everlasting, are happy on any soil provided it is sunny and on the dry side. They flower, with small crisp white blossoms from July to September.
Seeds may be sown outdoors in April and plants divide easily in early spring.

Arranging
This is a pretty little silver plant which can be used to tuck into small arrangements. The flower heads are useful as dried material for collage.

Preparation
A diagonal cut before plunging stem ends into boiling water for a few minutes, then give a long cool deep drink. To dry, hang up after removing all leaves.

Anemone japonica hybrid

Anemone

blanda	15 cm
fulgens	30 cm
hupehensis (japonica) AGM	90 cm
x 'Louise Uhink'	90 cm
x 'Queen Charlotte'	50 cm

Charming and varied, these herbaceous perennials all grow best in soil enriched with rotted manure or good compost.
A. blanda is happy in light shade, like our own wild wood anemones and may now be obtained in several colour shades. They all flower in early spring.
A. fulgens prefers more sunshine and comes into bloom in May, a wonderful scarlet at that season.
The japonica group, pink tones, like their roots in shade and their heads in filtered sunlight. This group is the latest to flower, going on well into the autumn, with single and semi-double flowers. They have fleshy roots and may be divided every three or four years or left undisturbed to increase on their own, enriched by a compost mulch in early spring before growth begins.
Plant *A. blanda* in autumn 5 cm deep and leave the roots to increase on their own. The plants will also make many seedlings.
A. fulgens should be set 7 cm deep in autumn or spring. On well drained soil the tubers may be left undisturbed for several years until they become too crowded.

Arranging
The japonica varieties are a good late summer flower particularly the white 'Louise Uhink', which combines well with white dahlias for September wedding arrangements and makes a useful alternative to white chrysanthemums.
A. fulgens gives a gay splash in the spring when red material is sparse. A few stems of *A. blanda* in a small cut glass vase bring spring into my house.
Anemones do not thrive in Oasis.

Preparation
A diagonal cut is often sufficient, otherwise a quick dip in boiling water before giving a long cool drink. Flower heads preserve in silica gel or borax.

Anthemis

cupaniana	30 cm
sancti-johannis	60 cm
tinctoria 'Mrs. E. C. Buxton' AGM	75 cm

Anthemis varieties are not particular about soil but

23

must have a sunny, well drained site, the smaller ones on patio or rock garden, the taller ones in a border.

A. cupaniana has low growing greyish aromatic cushions of leaves and white flowers with yellow centres. The other two varieties have yellow daisy flowers throughout the summer. 'Mrs. E. C. Buxton' is more lemon than gold shaded.

Clumps may be divided in March or shoots sprouting from the base may be rooted in spring. New plants can be raised from seed sown in April outdoors, but the plants will be variable in habit.

Arranging
These plants have pretty grey or green foliage which is most attractive when mixed with pink flowers.

Preparation
Diagonal cutting of stems.

perennials, we treat them here as half hardy annuals, raised from seed in heat in February or March, pricked out, hardened off and transplanted into open borders in April or May. They will produce gay splashes of varied colour from June until the autumn. Owing to rust disease, it is wise not to grow them in the same border two years running. The selected rust resistant strains now have very much clearer colours than used to be the case and are well worth a trial, specially in gardens where rust has occurred in previous seasons.

Arranging
These are excellent annuals either for arranging on their own or in large mixed summer vases.

Preparation
A diagonal cut and a long deep drink.

Hybrid antirrhinum

Aquilegia 'Nora Barlow'

Antirrhinum

majus 'Little Darling' dwarf selection	30 cm
rust resistant strains	35 cm

Although the snapdragons are really short lived

Aquilegia

alpina	30 cm
'Nora Barlow'	70cm
vulgaris 'McKana Hybrids'	90cm

Light, well drained soil with ample leaf-mould and a semi-shaded aspect is all these gracious columbine plants ask. They are not long lived perennials and division of old roots is not very satisfactory.

Better results are to be had by sowing seed of selected

strains in a cold frame or shady seed bed in April, to flower the following year. Self sown or home saved seedlings tend to revert to wild types and in the case of long spurred varieties, to lose their spurs.

A. alpina is a short spurred species of beautiful blue shade, flowering in May. The 'McKana Hybrids' come in many shades of red, purple and gold and flower in the summer months.

Arranging
With their delightful shapes and colours these flowers deserve to be used on their own. The most unusual flower heads of *A.* 'Nora Barlow', red-green, look very beautiful with just apple green foliage.

Preparation
Cut the stem ends and dip in boiling water for a few seconds, then give a long cool drink. Dry by hanging the heads upside down.

Armeria maritima (front) and bergenia

Armeria

maritima	25 cm
maritima 'Alba'	25 cm

Sandy loams on sunny borders are the favourite sites for these native thrifts, hardy perennials which are not herbaceous but carry their close, bright green clumps of foliage throughout the year and are attractive at all seasons.

The pink and white flower heads last for several months in the summer to make a very colourful edging or to provide groups on rock garden or patio. Established plants have a rootstock which is not easy to divide but short cuttings may be rooted in the protection of a cold frame in summer or autumn. Seed too, may be sown in a cold frame in spring.

Arranging
These little compact heads are a must for tiny arrangements.

Preparation
No special treatment.

Artemisia

absinthium 'Lambrook Silver'	AGM	90 cm
maritima 'Silver Queen'		75 cm
lactiflora		1·2 m
nutans		60 cm
schmidtiana 'Nana'		8 cm

Mostly grown for their attractive silvery foliage, these species thrive on any ordinary soil in an open, sunny site. However, there is one exception; for *A. lactiflora* to look its best and produce the fine plumes of creamy white flowers in late summer, it must have really good moist soil.

For patio work *A. schmidtiana* 'Nana' with dainty grey leaves and flowers is a delight. The other kinds will add contrast to a mixed bed or will fit happily into special grey borders.

Tall, herbaceous kinds divide easily in early spring. The grey-leafed ones will grow from cuttings but as felty stems are not always easy to propagate, it is often better to take a small sliver of older wood at the base of each cutting.

One plant from this group which may prove invasive is *A. maritima* and this needs to be kept in check. 'Lambrook Silver' should be pruned back in April like an evergreen shrub.

Arranging
These plants have such decorative foliage that no

flower arranger's garden should be without them. I think they look very attractive growing with the different coloured dianthus and that is also how I like to arrange them, my particular favourites being the pink and clove shades.

Preparation
Hammer and split stems or dip stem ends in boiling water and then place in deep cold water. Seed heads can be dried by hanging.

Artemisia schmidtiana 'Nana'

Arum

italicum pictum	45 cm
maculatum	25 cm

The first species which produces such handsome variegated green and cream foliage, needs a sheltered outdoor home and a covering of dry leaves in winter.
The second, the cuckoo pint or wild arum, prefers a shady glade as in its wild home.
Both may be increased from offsets in autumn and by seed sown in spring.
Arum leaves contain an irritant juice and the gay berries which hold the seeds are very poisonous if eaten.

Arranging
This plant is another must for the flower arranger's

garden. The leaves are most useful for completely concealing a pinholder at the base of a shallow dish arrangement and the lovely markings make the material a very attractive addition to spring flowers. The berries make an effective focal point in autumn groups.

Preparation
Submerge the leaves completely for twenty-four hours before using.

Arum italicum pictum and *Tiarella cordifolia*

Aster

acris		50 cm
amellus 'King George'	AGM	60 cm
x *frikartii*	AGM	80 cm
cordifolius 'Silver Spray'		90 cm
ericoides 'Brimstone'		80 cm
novi-belgii 'Little Pink Beauty'		40 cm

These herbaceous michaelmas daisies are in quite distinct groups, but to look their best all need good soil. The largest flowered – 'King George' and *A. frikartii* – have mildew resistant leaves and may be increased by spring cuttings in a cold frame or by division of clumps as growth begins.
A. acris is one of the first small flowered species to open followed closely by *A. cordifolius* with a dainty spray habit and *A. ericoides*. 'Little Pink Beauty' is best as an edging or in a patio.
All need dividing and replanting on fresh soil every

two or three years, always discarding the woody centres of old plants.

Arranging
I always think these flowers look most effective in harvest festival arrangements. They also make lovely additions to late summer mixed vases, particularly the blue-pink and the blue-mauve shades.

Preparation
Hammer stem ends and dip in boiling water for ten seconds, then give a long cool drink.

Aster novi-belgii 'Little Pink Beauty'

Arranging
These beautiful coloured spikes add such interest to large pedestal arrangements. They are often best used with the foliage stripped off. *A. x a.* 'Ostrich Plume' gives a striking arching effect for the sides of pedestals.

Preparation
Split or hammer the stems and dip ends in boiling water, followed by a long, deep, cool drink. Dry by hanging when the seed heads are really ripe.

Astilbes, planted in bold groups

Astilbe

x *arendsii* 'Bressingham Beauty'	90 cm
x *arendsii* 'Ostrich Plume'	75 cm
simplicifolia 'Sprite'	25 cm

All astilbes need deep, loamy soil in damp, semi-shaded situations beside a pond or stream. Planted with crown buds only just below the surface and given a good annual mulch of well rotted organic matter, they should thrive without disturbance for a number of years. Attractive both in lacy foliage and colourful flowers in warm white or rosy shades, they do not usually need staking.
The rootstock is always tough to handle when dividing crowns in early spring.
A. s. 'Sprite' begins to flower in early June, closely followed by the others, giving rich masses of colour until the autumn.

Astrantia

carniolica 'Rubra'	45 cm
major	80 cm
maxima variegata	60 cm

These unusual dainty flowers in shades of green, red and pink, love shady moist borders at the edge of a secluded path. They begin to flower in June and may continue well into the autumn.
Plants are easily divided in autumn or early spring and some may be raised from seed, but the resulting plants will vary in colour.

Arranging
This plant has rather a curious scent so only use it in

arrangements that are a little remote!

Preparation
A diagonal cut and a long cool drink in deep water.
Preserve by glycerine method.

Astrantia major

Aucuba japonica 'Variegata'

Aucuba

japonica 'Variegata'   2 m

Spotted laurel is a good natured, well tried evergreen
which grows in town or country and in sun or shade,
although the variegation is more marked if the shrub
be on a sunny site. Aucuba tolerates most soils and
makes a natural neat, rounded head. Any necessary
pruning should be done in April.
Berries may be stratified or hardwood cuttings set
outdoors in autumn.

Arranging
This variegated shrub has useful winter foliage when
there is very little available from the garden.

Preparation
Split or hammer stem ends and give a long cool deep
drink.

Azalea: see rhododendron

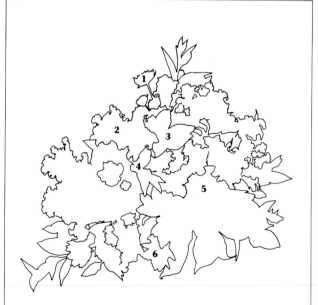

1 *Astrantia carniolica*
2 *Alchemilla mollis*
3 *Euonymus fortunei* 'Silver Queen'
4 *Hypericum* x *moserianum* 'Tricolor'
5 *Cornus alba* 'Elegantissima'
6 *Euonymus fortunei* 'Emerald 'n Gold'

Ballota

pseudodictamnus   60 cm

This useful grey-leafed plant is happy in a border or at the sunny edge of a group of shrubs. It is a true cut and come again plant.

It may be increased by heeled cuttings in July and young plants should have the protection of a cold frame for the first winter.

Trim mature plants back in May and the result will be a mound of fresh green shoots which grow taller and whiter as the summer comes.

Arranging
This is another of my favourite materials. The graceful curving sprays of soft grey leaves give such a pleasing line to many arrangements. Avoid getting the leaves wet because the greyish colour disappears.

Preparation
Cut and dip just the stem ends into boiling water, then give a long cool deep drink.

Ballota pseudodictamnus

Berberis thunbergii atropurpurea

Berberis

thunbergii AGM		60 cm
thunbergii atropurpurea AGM		60 – 90 cm
thunbergii 'Atropurpurea Nana' AGM		30 cm
wilsoniae AGM		1 – 1·5 m
darwinii AGM		1 – 2 m
x *stenophylla* AGM		2 m
verruculosa AGM		1 – 2 m

This is a large genus from which we have chosen seven of the best. All except *B. t.* 'Atropurpurea Nana' are thorny and can make good, natural hedges in any well drained soil and open situation.

The *B. thunbergii* and *B. wilsoniae* selections are at their best in autumn when brilliant leaves and berries often remain for several weeks. The evergreens, *B. darwinii* and *B.* x *stenophylla* are most handsome in spring at flowering time.

Pruning is not necessary except to remove straggling or invasive growth after flowering.

Berberis will grow from seed if berries are stratified in autumn and hard wood cuttings may be rooted outdoors.

Arranging
These are some of the most useful species to grow providing material, either foliage, flowers or berries for most of the year. There are so many colours available from the different varieties that they can be used in almost any kind of vase. Use the long arching sprays to give attractive shapes.

Preparation
Hammer or split the stem ends and strip off a little of the lower bark to encourage water absorption. Give a long drink in warm water.

Berberis darwinii

Bergenia

'Ballawley'	30 cm
cordifolia 'Purpurea'	30 cm
delavayi	30 cm
'Silberlicht' AGM	30 cm
'Sunningdale'	45 cm

These plants, on which both foliage and flowers are so valuable, will thrive in sun or shade on almost any soil and provide ground cover throughout the year. They divide readily after flowering.

Arranging
What beautiful foliage this plant has for arranging, supplying fresh looking leaves in winter when material is difficult to come by. These are excellent for using at the base of arrangements, their autumn colouring looking most effective when incorporated with pink and red flowers.

Preparation
Submerge for a few hours in cold water, then dry off and arrange.

Bergenia cordifolia

Buxus

sempervirens   2 m
sempervirens 'Latifolia Maculata'   2 m

These useful neat leafed evergreens which thrive so well on chalky soils can provide shelter and background for other less hardy plants.

Box bushes may be left to grow naturally or pruned as a hedge when they should be cut twice during the growing season. In the event of large branches having to be cut out, the work should be done in April.

Propagation is easy by division of small bushes or by layering or cuttings.

Arranging

A very useful glossy foliage which is readily available when most greenery is scarce. It shows off the first daffodils of spring very effectively.

Preparation

Hammer or split stem ends and give a good drink.

Calendula officinalis 'Fiesta Gitana'

Calendula

officinalis 'Fiesta Gitana'   30 cm

From among the many varieties of these popular marigolds, we have chosen a new selection with warm and varied orange shades. Seeds are best sown direct on a sunny border. Thinnings can be transplanted. Although the later flowers are smaller, the plants will flower throughout the summer if fading heads are cut off promptly. Self sown seedlings, the following year will be colourful but small in flower size.

Arranging

These are excellent flowers for cutting and giving a burst of colour indoors. I like them on their own in a brown pottery container or in a dark brown basket.

Preparation

A diagonal cut and then give a long, deep, cool drink.

Callicarpa

bodinieri giraldii   2 m

The amethyst berry, so called because of the attractive colour of its autumn fruits, is a neat, rather unusual shrub beloved for the purple shaded flowers and autumn foliage as well as the fruit. A warm, loamy soil on a sheltered border is needed.

Cut last year's flowered wood fairly hard back to low

Buxus sempervirens forms a neat hedge

buds in February or March to prevent the shrub becoming straggly and bare at the base.
Half ripened wood cuttings may be rooted in a cold frame.

Arranging
This is rather a nice shrub to use in autumn when it has large clusters of deep purple berries which add interest to a bowl of mauve asters or michaelmas daisies.

Preparation
Hammer or split stem ends then give a long cool drink.

Callicarpa bodinieri giraldii

Campanula

alliariifolia 'Ivory Bells'	50 cm
carpatica 'Blue Moonlight'	25 cm
glomerata 'Joan Elliott'	45 cm
lactiflora 'Loddon Anna' AGM	1·3 m
latiloba	90 cm
persicifolia 'Telham Beauty' AGM	1 m

A wonderful summer collection of bell flowers is available to us and it is heartening to know that they will thrive in any good garden soil in sunny or shady situations.

In herbaceous borders, stake plants early so that the tall varieties grow through the stakes and are supported by them.
Perennial varieties divide easily in autumn, after flowering, or in spring as growth begins.

Arranging
What pretty flowers these are in so many shades of blue, and now in pink and white. Arrange in vases which allow enough room for their real beauty to be seen.

Preparation
Hammer the woody stems, otherwise split or diagonal cut and give a long cool drink.

Campanula persicifolia 'Alba'

Caryopteris

clandonensis AGM	1 m

This dainty little shrub produces welcome blue spikes in late summer and is sometimes called the blue spiraea. It thrives in a sunny spot and is happy on warm, well drained soils, including chalky areas.

Prune it like *Buddleia davidii* in February or early March, cutting back the stems which flowered the previous summer to low buds. Often new growth does not start until May.

Cuttings of young shoots root readily in a cold frame in summer. It may also be grown from seed.

Arranging

I came across this shrub by accident and what luck, for it is so very useful in the autumn with bowls of pink and mauve flowers.

Preparation

It is very important to split the stems and make sure they have taken up water before using. Then give a long cool drink. At any sign of wilting, recut and split afresh.

Caryopteris clandonensis (front) with *Berberis thunbergii* 'Rose Glow'

Centaurea

dealbata 'John Coutts' AGM		60 cm
hypoleuca		30 cm
macrocephala		1·2 m
cyanus 'Polka Dot' strain		45 cm
moschata (sweet sultan)		45 cm

This wide ranging genus which includes both annual and perennial species thrives on sunny, well drained sites.

Perennials may be divided in early spring, while the annual cornflower *C. cyanus* and sweet sultan can be sown indoors in March for later pricking out and transplanting, or outdoors in April on the site where they are to flower.

Arranging

Be sure to gather these flowers before they are fully open, otherwise they rapidly fade. Now there is such a variety of colours these species make very useful cut flowers to put in groups in arrangements.

Preparation

Lightly hammer the stem ends and give a long deep drink. The flower heads will dry naturally on the plant.

Centaurea dealbata 'John Coutts'

Chaenomeles

japonica AGM		1 – 2 m
speciosa 'Moerloosii' AGM		1 – 2 m

Hardy and accommodating as to soil and aspect, it is not surprising that the lovely Japanese quince is one of our favourite garden shrubs. It will grow happily against a wall, even facing north or east, or may be left to develop as a natural bush.

Free growing bushes need no regular pruning, in fact

the thicker the branches grow together, the less buds seem to be taken by the bullfinches. Trained bushes need long new shoots pruning hard back in autumn. These bushes produce golden fruits in autumn which make splendid jelly as well as being decorative in themselves.

The species may be grown from stratified seed or half ripened wood cuttings can be rooted in a cold frame.

Arranging
Little sprigs of this shrub in flower can be used, but I also find that long, new shoots pruned out make extremely good foliage for backgrounds in large containers.

Preparation
Hammer and split the stems and then give a really good long drink.

Chamaecyparis lawsoniana 'Stewartii'

Chamaecyparis

lawsoniana	4 – 5 m
lawsoniana 'Stewartii'	2 m

Lawson's cypress was introduced to Great Britain from the United States of America well over a century ago. Hardy and adaptable, it has become a firm favourite as a graceful specimen tree or as a wind break or hedge. Its deep green foliage is a wonderful background for flowering shrubs. When grown as a formal hedge, clipping should be begun at an early age for it will look far neater when young growth is regularly trimmed than if pruning is delayed until stems become hard and woody.

Growth in this species is steady and the habit is more spreading than in the fastigiate cultivars. In favoured localities the tree will grow far taller than the height indicated and should therefore not be planted too near to buildings.

Many cultivars (varieties) of Lawson's cypress are now catalogued, some with silvery, feathery, bluish or golden foliage, others columnar, dwarf or spreading. A visit to a good nursery or garden centre will reveal the wide choice available. For smaller gardens, choose from among the dwarfer cultivars.

Chaenomeles (quince)

C.l. 'Stewartii' our other selection, with rich golden foliage, is rather more spreading than the type and will not ultimately grow so tall. It should be grown as a specimen tree in an open situation. The beauty of form would be lost if it were grown as a hedge.

Pet cats and dogs can cause burning to the lower foliage of any cypress or other conifer. This can be avoided by protecting the base of the conifer with a few plants of a low growing species such as *Ruta graveolens,* the odour of which is said to repel all animals except the weasel.

If growing *C. lawsoniana* as a hedge, trim with secateurs.

Plant bushes in September or April either from balled sacking or from containers, preferably starting with small plants as these have a much better chance of surviving in a new environment.

Please refer to the section on planting shrubs for note about spraying evergreens.

Hard wood, heeled cuttings, taken in autumn will root fairly readily in open ground.

Arranging
A material that is always available throughout the whole year in such a variety of greens and golds. You can either use large pieces as a background for the big groups, or cut very small pieces and use them to fill in in smaller arrangements.

Preparation
Either hammer or split stem ends and give a good drink.

Preparation
Hammer or split stem ends then give a good long cold drink. Preserve by glycerine method.

Choisya ternata

Choisya

ternata	2 m

This Mexican orange plant thrives in sheltered borders either among other shrubs or against a wall or fence; its evergreen foliage always looks attractive. Add peat or leaf-mould to the soil when planting.

No regular pruning is needed: straggly shoots may be cut back after flowering.

Spring cuttings of soft wood will root in gentle heat.

Arranging
This shrub has really fresh looking green foliage which makes a perfect foil for spring flowers such as daffodils. It can also be used in May when its clusters of attractive white flowers will enhance a green and white arrangement.

Chrysanthemum

coccineum	60 cm
'Korean Hybrids'	90 cm
maximum 'Esther Read'	60 cm

All these species give best results if planted in really good soil in an open, sunny plot. *C. coccineum,* better known as pyrethrum is an early herbaceous perennial filling a gap at the end of May.

It may be divided immediately after flowering. *C. maximum* may be divided in early spring and Korean chrysanthemums, bronze, gold and apricot shades, may be raised from seed the first year, the best plants selected and subsequently increased by soft wood cuttings from the clumps rooted in heat in spring.

Arranging
This is a very long lasting genus which is so useful to

the flower arranger. The white flowers of *C.* 'Esther Read' are a wonderful asset as they can be used on their own or added to a large wedding arrangement if there is a great demand for white flowers.

Preparation
Gently hammer stem ends and give a deep long cold drink.

give height and an interesting shape to arrangements at a time when the flowers of other tall plants of similar habit are over.

Preparation
Dip stem ends in boiling water for a few seconds then give a long deep cold drink.

Chrysanthemum maximum

Cimicifuga, an unusual addition to a herbaceous bed

Cimicifuga

racemosa   1·2 m

Moist, shady conditions are best for this graceful herbaceous perennial which flowers in July and August. Roots may be divided in spring or seed may be sown in a cold frame.

Arranging
The tall spikes of ivory blossoms on shiny black stems

Clarkia

elegans   60 cm

From a direct sowing outdoors in April, this favourite annual will provide colour and material for cutting from July onwards. Fine twigs among the plants at an early stage will help to keep stems upright.

Arranging
These long lasting flowers have such pretty pastel shades that I often arrange them on their own in pewter or in a grey container. Gather when the

37

flowers are open down almost the entire length of the stem.

Preparation
Remove all greenery below the water line. Dip stem ends in boiling water and then give a good long cool drink.

Clematis

alpina 'Columbine'	2 m
armandii AGM	6 – 8 m
integrifolia	75 cm
macropetala AGM	2 m
montana rubens AGM	5 – 6 m
'Nelly Moser' AGM	2 m
orientalis	5 m
tangutica	3 m

All clematis benefit by being rather deeply planted and having moist soil with shady conditions at the roots while flowering growths are in sunlight. Species often prove easier to grow than large flowered varieties and among those we have chosen C. 'Nelly Moser' is the only large flowered variety.

The species *C. armandii* is not quite hardy and its evergreen foliage needs the protection of a warm wall.

C. integrifolia makes an interesting contribution to the herbaceous border and can be increased by division.

The climbing species, some of which are very vigorous, can romp over outhouses, through shrubs or up walls among other trained shrubs. We have *C. montana rubens* climbing to the gable, while *C. tangutica* happily scrambles through *Prunus cerasifera* 'Pissardii' its yellow flowers and fluffy seed heads lighting the sombre purple foliage of its host.

Pruning varies with the species. Generally speaking spring flowering species are trimmed back after flowering. Later varieties, which bloom on new wood, need cutting back to plump, low buds in February or early March.

Always buy clematis in pots and to encourage extra root formation and new bud development below ground, earth up stems a little after planting.

Cuttings of young wood, taken in May or June may sometimes be rooted indoors. They are usually taken internodally and species are easier to root than large flowered varieties. Layering can be successful and species may be grown from seed sown as soon as it ripens.

Arranging
Many flower arrangers discount clematis, but if treated

properly they will last for a few days. I either float the heads in a glass bowl or use a few blooms as a focal point in an arrangement. Stems of the smaller flowered varieties can be used to drape over the edges of a pedestal.

Preparation
If floating the heads, lightly crush the stems, which should be short; they can then be quickly dipped in boiling water, taking care to protect the flower and then given a long cold drink. Seed heads can be left to dry naturally on the plant.

Clerodendron trichotomum

Clerodendron

bungei (foetidum)	1·5 m
trichotomum AGM	2 – 3 m

Hardy shrubs which came to us from China and Japan, the clerodendrons ask little but good soil. Pruning is seldom required.

New plants may be raised from seed stratified and sown in spring or by half ripened wood cuttings in a cold frame in August.

The shrubs are late flowering and fragrant; in addition the blue berries of *C. trichotomum* held in crimson calyces are an autumn feature.

Arranging
I feel this shrub is rather neglected as material for flower arranging and this is a pity. I use it mainly with the leaves removed to reveal the beautiful white flower sprays and think it well worth growing.

Preparation
Hammer or split the stem ends and give a long deep cold drink.

Cobaea

scandens   up to 10 m

This fast growing climber is perennial by nature but usually treated as an annual, raised from seed sown in heat in spring and planted out in light soil in June beside a wall or trellis or among shrubs.

Arranging
This quaint bell-shaped flower makes a lovely addition to a summer arrangement if tucked into the centre. When the trumpets are green they look beautiful introduced into an all green arrangement.

Preparation
A diagonal cut and then a drink of warm water keeping the heads propped up out of the water.

Colutea

arborescens   3 m

This little bush, the bladder senna, will adapt to poor soil or dry areas on banks where many other shrubs would fail and its racemes of yellow flowers in summer are followed by inflated, tinted seed pods.
It is only pruned to take out weak shoots or to shorten straggling branches during November.
Easily raised from seed sown outdoors in spring, it may also be grown from hard wood cuttings set outside in autumn.

Arranging
Interest in this plant is provided by the pale green pods which are splashed with red or copper in late September and are rather effective for complementing autumn berry and fruit arrangements.

Preparation
Hammer stem ends and give a long cold drink.

Colutea arborescens

Convallaria

majalis 'Rosea'   20 cm
majalis 'Flore Pleno'   20 cm

These early, summer flowers, varieties of the well-loved lily of the valley, grow a little taller than the type but need the same treatment: good soil in light shade or for early flowers, a warm south-facing corner.
Replant the roots every four years or so, working fresh organic matter into the soil.
The plants may be increased by division of the crowns or from seed from the red autumn berries. (Do remember these berries are poisonous and keep them out of reach of children).
Clumps of crowns may be lifted in early spring, potted and brought indoors to flower several weeks early.

Arranging

What a dainty little flower this is, with such a pleasant scent. I tend to gather the flower spikes with a few leaves and placing the foliage round the outside of the bunch, pop them straight into a simple china vase deep enough to hold the stems slightly upright.

Preparation

If you are not going to arrange these flowers straight away they will keep their freshness if placed in cold water.

Cornus alba 'Sibirica'

Coreopsis grandiflora hybrid

Coreopsis

grandiflora		60 cm
verticillata	AGM	60 cm

These gay perennial daisies need a sunny, well drained border. They flower in early summer.
Seed may be sown outdoors in April or plants can be divided in early spring.

Arranging

Because of the strong yellow petal colour of coreopsis, these slender stemmed daisies make a nice focal point in mixed summer arrangements.

Preparation

Hammer stem ends and give a long cool drink.

Cornus

alba 'Elegantissima'	AGM	1·5 – 2 m
alba 'Sibirica'		2 m
alba 'Spaethii'	AGM	1·5 – 2 m
stolonifera 'Flaviramea'	AGM	2 m
florida		2 m
florida rubra	AGM	2 m
kousa		5 m
kousa chinensis	AGM	2 – 3 m
mas	AGM	3 m
nuttallii		8 – 10 m

These two groups of dogwoods each have their special values in the garden. The group including C. *alba* and C. *stolonifera* are loved particularly for their brilliantly coloured bark in winter.
They should be pruned hard back in early spring to

encourage new basal shoots, the best colour being always on young wood. *C. a.* 'Spaethii' has golden variegated foliage in summer and *C. a.* 'Elegantissima' is variegated white and green. This group is fairly easy to grow, thriving in most soils, including chalky areas. It also tolerates sun or shade or sites near the water's edge.

Species in the second group, however, need good deep soil and only extensive gardens would have room for the taller varieties. With the exception of *Cornus mas,* which has small yellow flowers before the leaves in early spring, these species have colourful flower-like bracts in late spring or early summer and rich hues in their autumn foliage.

Cornus species can be increased by hard wood cuttings in autumn or by layering.

Arranging

What an asset these bare, beautifully coloured stems are on drab winter days. I use them to make a line arrangement with a few flowers. The early flowers of *C. mas* will enhance a spring arrangement of daffodils. *C. florida* and its pink form also produce flowering stems in the summer which are useful for large arrangements.

Preparation

Hammer or split stem ends and give an overnight drink in cold water.

Corylus

avellana 'Contorta'	2 m
maxima 'Purpurea'	2 m

These hardy hazel bushes thrive in sun or shade on good deep loam. They need less protection than many shrubs. Both bear nuts from which new plants can be raised.

The first species makes a remarkable screen with its twisted branches and is specially lovely when the catkins open in spring.

The second species is a fine purple background for golden or grey-leafed shrubs in summer. We grow a rich purple clematis through the bush with fine effect.

No regular pruning is necessary as neither shrub is rampant.

Arranging

C. a. 'Contorta' is a small tree that once used proves indispensable. In winter it makes an interesting background for early spring daffodils. *C. m.* 'Purpurea' provides rich purple foliage to set off pale mauve or

pink flowers in summer arrangements.

Preparation

Peel off the lowest 3 cm of bark and hammer stem ends. Give a warm drink, then a long cool one.

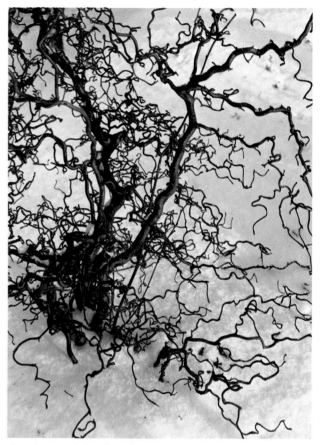

Corylus avellana 'Contorta'

Cosmos

(Cosmea) 'Sensation Mixed'	90 cm

Our selection is a single variety of this half hardy annual. It may be sown indoors in February or March for transplanting in May, or outdoors in late April. It likes best a warm, well drained border.

Arranging

This is another useful daisy-like flower in crimson, pink and white shades, which lasts well in mixed summer vases and has a long flowering period.

Preparation

Lightly hammer the stem ends and give a long cold drink.

Cotinus

americanus	3 m
coggygria	3 m
coggygria 'Foliis Purpureis Notcutt's Variety'	2 m

Now separated from the rhus genus, the cotinus species do best on light sandy loam and are valued for their smoky summer flower heads and the brilliant autumn foliage colouring. The last named variety is resplendent throughout the summer with rich purple foliage.

No pruning is needed unless to trim back an over vigorous branch. Shoots may be layered in autumn.

Arranging

Do not try to use this foliage when it is too young. The dainty puffs of smoke (flower heads) which *C. coggygria* produces add interest if tucked into an arrangement. These shrubs are mainly used for the wonderful autumn leaf colours. The branches make a splendid foil for berries and for the red and bronze dahlias.

Preparation

Place stem ends into 3 cm of boiling water for at least five minutes, then submerge the entire branches in cold water overnight.

Cotinus coggygria hybrid

Cotoneaster

'Cornubia'	AGM	5–6 m
frigidus		5 m
horizontalis	AGM	2 m
lacteus		3 m
simonsii		2 m
wardii		2 m

Coming mainly from China and the Himalayas during the past century, these hardy shrubs can find a place in almost all our gardens. They are not fussy about soil, the taller ones make good wind-breaks and hedges, the shorter ones such as *C. horizontalis* will adapt as a mounded shrub or grow against fence or wall. Every species has attractive autumn berries and cream or white flowers. Except when grown as hedges, pruning is not needed.

The species hybridise readily. Seed may be stratified in autumn to germinate outdoors in spring. Hard wood cuttings may also be taken in autumn.

Arranging

What better foliage could you ask for to provide all types of lines, both formal and informal in arrangements. Then there are the added advantages of interesting coloured leaves, flowers and berries.

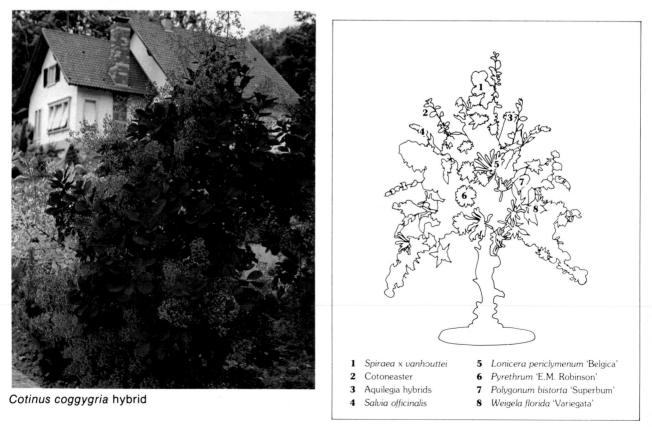

1	*Spiraea* x *vanhouttei*	**5**	*Lonicera periclymenum* 'Belgica'
2	Cotoneaster	**6**	*Pyrethrum* 'E.M. Robinson'
3	Aquilegia hybrids	**7**	*Polygonum bistorta* 'Superbum'
4	*Salvia officinalis*	**8**	*Weigela florida* 'Variegata'

Preparation
Stem ends of flowering branches should be dipped in boiling water for two minutes and then given a long cold drink.

Cotoneaster creating a magnificent display

Crataegus monogyna 'Pendula'

Crataegus

monogyna	8 m
oxyacantha 'Paul's Scarlet' AGM	5 m

Good soil in shrub border or on a lawn will suit these hardy hawthorns. *C. monogyna* is still among the best hedging plants and as a hedge needs clipping twice a year before the spiny shoots grow tough. Grown as specimen bushes, pruning is not needed except to keep the tree shapely.

Seed of white thorn may be stratified when it will germinate in the second year. Scarlet thorn is usually grafted.

Arranging
These are underrated trees that come out with such lovely pink or white blossoms to add beauty to a large arrangement in late spring.

Preparation
Hammer the stem ends and put in warm water.

Crocosmia

'Lucifer'	1 m
'Bressingham Blaze'	75 cm

These new hardy hybrids rather like large montbretias, need good, light soil in a warm border. If you garden on heavy land, plant the corms in a trowel full of coarse sand, 15 cm deep in autumn. Replant the groups every three or four years and at this time offsets may be taken off and set in a nursery bed.

Seed may also be saved and sown in a cold frame but will take several years to form flowering corms.

Arranging
These are long lasting flowers of intense orange shades. The arching stems give a good outline for autumn arrangements when a large number of flat headed flowers have been included.

Preparation
A diagonal cut and a good long drink. Leaves can be preserved by the glycerine method or they can be pressed. The flower seed heads dry naturally on the plant.

Crocosmia masonorum fronted by sedum

Crocus

biflorus
chrysanthus
sieberi
speciosus
tomasinianus

These little species, which seldom grow taller than 10 cm have given rise to many lovely varieties. Light soil in borders or in grass is best. Plant in autumn (August for *C. speciosus*) and leave the corms undisturbed. In the main, the species increase naturally by seed and tiny corms. Twigs with black cotton stretched across, before crocus flower, will ward off marauding birds in spring.

Never cut the leaves off until they are completely dried up if you wish the corms to increase in numbers.

Arranging

As with so many small spring flowers, crocus look best in moss gardens on slabs of wood, the containers being concealed by moss.

Preparation

A diagonal cut.

Cytisus

albus (multiflorus)	AGM	2 m
battandieri	AGM	3 – 4 m
x *praecox*	AGM	1 – 2 m
scoparius		2 m

An open site, neutral and deep soils, even clayey loams will suit this genus best but none, save *C. battandieri,* is long lived. Prune *C. albus, C.* x *praecox* and *C. scoparius* immediately after flowering, cutting back the shoots which have flowered, to the lowest buds. The bushes will remain well covered for five or six years, after which time they tend to die back or get blown over. Brooms should be bought in pots to begin with as the roots dislike disturbance.

Cuttings of young wood may be rooted in summer in a cold frame. Seeds may be sown, but may not come true. They may, however, produce very interesting hybrid plants.

Prune *C. battandieri* to low buds in early spring.

Arranging

With such white, cream and golden colours it is a shame that this plant, when in full flower, will not last long in water. However, stems can be used for a few days and they do give a flowing line to an arrangement. The foliage is always useful and many people like it for its strong curves, these keeping their shape once moulded.

Preparation

Dip stem ends in boiling water for a few minutes then give a long cold drink. Or just hammer the ends and give a good drink. Moulding can be done either under water or by curling the stems round the inside of a saucepan and leaving overnight.

Cytisus praecox creating a focal point

Dahlia

pom-pom and decorative varieties   50 – 90 cm

All dahlias like an open situation and good soil. Although in milder areas tubers survive the winter underground, elsewhere it is safer to lift and store them in bags or boxes in a frost-proof place. A little soil left on the tubers is an advantage. In March, if the tubers are brought into a warm place, bedded in soil or moist peat, shoots soon sprout and may be used as cuttings which are rooted indoors for planting out in late May.

Dahlias may also be raised from seed sown indoors in March and there is an increasing range from which to choose in any good catalogue.

Arranging

I rather think I prefer dahlias arranged on their own,

as there are so many shades available. If you do use them with other material try to choose flowers of a contrasting shape.

Preparation

Dip stem ends into boiling water and then give a good long cool drink. Pom-poms can be preserved with silica gel.

Danae

racemosa (Ruscus racemosus)   60 cm

Planted in autumn under trees in any moist soil, this little evergreen should thrive. Prune out any dead, brown shoots in April.

It can be increased by seed stratified in autumn or by division in spring.

Arranging
This useful foliage cuts very well and makes a polished green background. After hot summers the berries produced add charm to autumn arrangements.

Preparation
Hammer or split the stem ends and give a long cold drink.

often finds seedlings coming up near the parent plant. Fragrant and beautiful as these shrubs are, it must be remembered that all their parts are poisonous and daphne is not therefore suitable for planting where children play.

Arranging
I enjoy using these plants for the beautiful scent they bring to a warm room and for this reason I try to add a few pieces of daphne to most spring arrangements.

Preparation
Either hammer the stem ends or place them in boiling water for a few minutes. Then give a long drink.

Daphne mezereum

Daphne

cneorum	30 cm
laureola	60 cm
mezereum AGM	1 – 1·5 m
mezereum 'Alba'	1 – 1·5 m
pontica	60 cm

Whether on open borders or in rock gardens, these shrubs appreciate peat in light, well drained soil.
No pruning is needed. Shoots may be layered in autumn or seed sown outdoors as soon as ripe. One

Delphinium ajacis

Delphinium

ajacis	70 cm
'Pacific Giants'	1·5m
'Pink Sensation'	90 cm

Both the annual larkspur, *D. ajacis* and the perennial hybrids need good rich loam on an open site to flower well. Sow larkspur outdoors in April and plant the perennials in autumn or spring, allowing 1 m between the plants. Stake firmly and early, and cut dead heads off after flowering. Top dress generously with organic matter to maintain the quality of the flower spikes and transplant roots to a new well prepared site every three years. Slugs can be a problem as the young shoots start growing. Weathered soot round the crowns, or a form of slug bait will help to prevent damage.

Named varieties can be grown from plant division in early spring or from soft cuttings of young shoots about 10 cm long, rooted indoors. New stock can be grown from seed sown between April and June for flowering the following year.

Arranging

I only use the tall hybrids for large groups such as wedding pedestal arrangements. The smaller ones fit very well in mixed summer vases.

Preparation

Remove all greenery below water line and then invert flower spike, fill hollow stem with water and plug with cotton wool. Smaller stemmed varieties can be lightly hammered and given a long cold drink. Hang flower heads upside down to dry or dry ripe seed heads upright.

Deutzia gracilis

Deutzia

gracilis	60 cm
x elegantissima AGM	1·5 m

These dainty, free flowering shrubs are happy in filtered shade on any good soil.

Prune the flowered shoots back to low buds straight after the flowers fade, to avoid bare stems the next year.

Plants can be increased by half ripened summer cuttings in a cold frame or by hard wood cuttings in the open ground in autumn.

Arranging

The big advantage of deutzia is that it is in flower when many similar shrubs are already over. Its dainty white or pink blossoms make it a sheer delight to use in early summer arrangements.

Preparation

Hammer stem ends well and then give a long cool drink.

Dianthus

barbatus	45 cm
'Crimson Treasure'	15 cm
'Doris'	30 cm
'Excelsior'	20 cm
'Mrs. Sinkins'	20 cm
'Pink Bouquet'	15 cm
rock hybrids	15 cm

Well drained soil and a sunny situation in border, patio or rock garden, will suit all these dianthus. They are also happy on limy soils. *D. barbatus,* the sweet william, is a biennial raised from seed sown in June to flower the following year. It has a long flowering season. The named varieties of dianthus and the rock hydrids can be layered in August or increased by cuttings of non-flowering shoots set in a cold frame in summer.

D. 'Crimson Treasure' and *D.* 'Pink Bouquet' form colourful grey patches of foliage which are attractive all through the winter.

Arranging

There are times when I wonder what we would do without dianthus. The little rock hybrids are best in miniature arrangements. Pinks look lovely with feathery grey foliage and the scented varieties give an extra bonus. I also like to use pinks in raised groups on dinner tables. Sweet williams are flowers I enjoy using to fill a basket.

Preparation
A diagonal cut and a long cold drink. The stem ends of sweet william should be lightly hammered and all greenery below the water line removed.

Garden pinks for a border edge in a sunny spot

Dicentra

eximia	20 cm
formosa 'Bountiful'	30 cm
spectabilis	50 cm

Semi-shade, good deep soil and space in which to grow without crowding are the essentials needed by this herbaceous genus. They are attractive both in foliage and flower, *D. spectabilis* being outstanding over a long period each year once it settles down.

The first two species divide readily in the winter months but *D. spectabilis* is more difficult as the rootstock is fleshy and very spreading. If care is taken, new shoots which form on the root each autumn may be taken with a short piece of root attached and set in a cold frame for planting out in spring. Flowering plants should not be disturbed once they have settled.

Arranging
The beautiful arching sprays of miniature pink or red and white lockets are perfect for the arranger. The natural curves give an attractive outline for many different arrangements.

Preparation
Dip stem ends in boiling water for five seconds, then give a long cold deep drink.

Dicentra formosa 'Bountiful' backed by yellow oenothera and blue aconitum

Digitalis

ambigua (grandiflora)	60 cm
x *mertonensis*	70 cm
purpurea 'Excelsior'	1 – 1·2 m
Sutton's 'Apricot'	1 m

These short lived perennials grow happily in filtered sunlight in deep loamy soils and are usually treated as biennial plants. The seed is sown in spring or early summer either outdoors or in a cold frame. Seedlings are subsequently transplanted to a nursery bed and in autumn or spring placed in their flowering position.

Arranging
These flowers, in shades of cream, pink, purple and

apricot, always remind me of cottage gardens, so I like to use them as naturally as possible and put them in large mixed summer vases.

Preparation

Place stem ends in warm water and give a long drink. Seed heads can be dried by hanging them upside down after removing all greenery.

Doronicum

plantagineum 'Harpur Crewe'   80 cm

This gay spring flowering perennial makes its welcome appearance with the narcissi and grows happily in shady or open borders.
Roots may be divided in autumn or spring. The plants quickly die down after flowering.

Arranging

The advantage of this gay golden daisy is the early flowering period, which makes it a nice addition to mixed spring vases.

Preparation

A diagonal cut and a long warm drink.

Digitalis purpurea

Echinops ritro

Echinacea

purpurea   1 m

In any sunny herbaceous border, this plant, the purple cone flower, has a charm of its own.
Plants may be divided in early spring or seed may be sown outdoors in April.

Arranging
Whenever a really erect flower is required in summer mixed arrangements, this solves the problem with its rose-red heads.

Preparation
Hammer stem ends lightly and give a long cool drink.

Echinacea purpurea

Echinops

ritro   1·1 m

Globe thistles all add interesting form to the herbace-ous border. They are beloved of bees and flower over several weeks. Any sunny border will suit them; they will also thrive in filtered shade.
Plants may be divided in early spring or seed sown outdoors in April.

Arranging
I thoroughly enjoy using these small neat blue-headed thistles, particularly in line arrangements.

Preparation
Hammer stems and give a good drink. Dry by hanging unripe heads upside down after defoliating. Leaves can be pressed.

Echium

vulgare   60 cm

A cousin of anchusa and forget-me-not, this biennial is suited in either a sunny border or a woodland, semi-shaded area.
Sow the seed in April outdoors and transplant in autumn to flowering quarters.

Arranging
I cannot understand why this plant seems to be grown less and less, as the beautiful dense blue-violet spikes last so well in water and provide an attractive colour to use in mixed summer vases.

Preparation
Dip stem ends in boiling water for one minute then give a long drink.

Elaeagnus

x *ebbingei*   AGM   3 m
macrophylla   AGM   3 m
pungens 'Maculata'   AGM   2 m

These shrubs which come to us from the Far East, thrive in any good, well drained soil, including those over chalk. All are evergreen and have fragrant flowers, the last named species being particularly cheerful in winter with its gold-splashed foliage. They may be used as specimen bushes or as wind-breaks or hedges.
Prune straggling branches or any which revert from variegated to green form. Plants may be set in early autumn or April. Layers may root in spring or half ripened cuttings in summer in a cold frame may be

successful. It is not the easiest genus to propagate.

material at times when flowers are scarce.

Arranging

E. p. 'Maculata' is wonderful winter material with its green and shining gold foliage providing an arrangement in itself and blending so well with the first spring flowers. Elaeagnus can be mixed in with other green

Preparation

Hammer stem ends or dip in boiling water. To preserve, place the hammered stem ends in a glycerine solution for a few weeks.

Elaeagnus pungens 'Maculata', one of the most useful variegated evergreen shrubs

Eranthis

hyemalis   8 cm
x tubergenii   8 – 12 cm

Winter aconites are happy in grass under deciduous trees or near the edges of shrub borders where shade is not too dense. The tubers, set to 6 – 8 cm deep in autumn, should be left undisturbed once they are planted. *E. hyemalis* seeds freely in areas where it is happy. *E.* x *tubergenii* is a hybrid and is seldom known to set seed.

Arranging
These lovely splashes of yellow are a must for the miniature spring garden arrangement in a dish or on a slab of wood.

Preparation
A diagonal cut and a good drink.

Eremurus

robustus   2 – 3 m
stenophyllus (bungei)   1 m

The rather fragile spreading roots of these asphodels, members of the lily family, will only succeed in deep rich loam which has been very well prepared. The plants need sunlight, ample moisture in dry spells and a mulch of well rotted organic matter round, but not on, the crowns, in early spring. They also need a good background to show up the pink and golden flower spikes to advantage. Once established they do not like to be disturbed.
Plant 15 cm deep to start with and protect the crowns in winter with light litter of bracken. Flower stems may need staking in summer.
Seed, when obtainable, may be sown in heat in spring. It may be slow to germinate and seedlings will be four to five years old before starting to flower.

Arranging
What a blessing the tall pale pink spikes of *E. robustus* are for large groups in church or marquee. *E. stenophyllus* is a smaller variety so it can be used in mixed summer vases in the house.

Preparation
A diagonal cut and a good drink.

Eremurus robustus

Erigeron

speciosus   50 cm

This is a parent of many newer varieties providing a succession of delicate pastel shaded flowers from May to October. They all prefer open sites on sunny borders with ample moisture at the roots. Plant the roots in the border in autumn or spring and trim stems back after flowering.
Named varieties may be divided in early spring or seed may be sown outdoors in spring, when the mixed seedlings will flower the following and subsequent years.

Arranging

These are long lasting daisies which show up very well in mixed summer arrangements.

Preparation

Dip stem ends in boiling water for a few minutes then give a long drink.

Erigeron (back) a useful flower for summer arrangements

Eryngium

alpinum AGM	75 cm
amethystinum	80 cm
giganteum	1 – 1·2 m
maritimum	60 cm
proteiflorum	50 cm

The sea holly, in all its forms, needs an open site on light, well drained soil. Striking tinted stems and foliage rival the attraction of the flowers themselves.
E. giganteum only flowers once and should be treated as a biennial. (It provides ample seed for sowing outdoors for subsequent years).
Others may also be sown outdoors in spring, or root cuttings may be taken in autumn or spring.
E. proteiflorum is a less well known but handsome species from Mexico where it grows high above the tree line. Some protection from excess damp is necessary in wet areas of this country. Seedlings need

the dry conditions of a cold frame until they are established.

Arranging

The subtle blues of sea holly species and their fine, stiff stems are a real joy for the flower arranger either used on their own or as a backcloth to pale pink or red flowers. A few of the larger heads can make a dramatic focal point.

Preparation

A diagonal cut then a good long drink. Blown heads can be preserved by the glycerine method or leaves may be removed and stems hung upside down to dry.

Eryngium alpinum

Escallonia

'C. F. Ball'	3 m
'Donard Seedling'	3 m
'Iveyi'	2 m
'Langleyensis' AGM	2 m
macrantha	4 m

This genus from South America is invaluable to us for its long flowering period in summer and autumn. It is happy and fairly hardy in any well drained soil, especially near the sea, and will also grow on chalky areas. Protection from a wall may be desirable in more northern areas.
The bushes are almost evergreen and if hard pruning

is ever needed, should be carried out in April. Otherwise trimming after flowering is all that is needed. Plant first in October or March. Half ripened wood cuttings may be rooted in a cold frame. Hybrids may also be raised from seed.
E. 'Donard Seedling' and E. 'Langleyensis' will make good hedges. E. 'Iveyi' with its white blossom shows up best against a dark wall.

Arranging
The arching dainty sprays of crimson, rose-pink and white flowers produce very graceful lines in all arrangements. They look their best when displayed with pink and white blooms, such as roses.

Preparation
Hammer stem ends or dip them in boiling water. Then give a good long drink.

Escallonia

Eucalyptus

gunnii	8 m
parviflora	6 m
perriniana	5 m

These three hardy species should be planted from pots in spring and need good average soil. *E. parviflora* will tolerate lime.
Protect young plants during the first two winters and cut back to about 40 cm. If the plants are treated as bushes, and kept cut, they will be less top heavy and will provide more suitable material for flower arrangements. Seed may be sown in heat in spring.

Arranging
These are among my favourite foliage plants. I love the glaucous grey leaf colour and the fact that normally the leafy stems are available all the year round. I like best to arrange them with red or pink flowers. It really is worth nurturing in the early years to get the plants established.

Preparation
Hammer stem ends or dip in boiling water and give a long drink. Preserve by the glycerine method.

Eucalyptus gunnii

Euonymus europaeus

Euonymus

europaeus	AGM	4 m
fortunei (radicans) 'Silver Queen'		2 m
fortunei (radicans) 'Emerald Gaiety'		30 cm
fortunei (radicans) 'Emerald 'n Gold'		30 cm
japonicus		2 m
sachalinensis (planipes)	AGM	3 m

This genus includes deciduous and evergreen species and is invaluable in some way to every garden. The deciduous species *E. europaeus* and *E. sachalinensis* provide colourful pink and orange fruits and rich autumn foliage; they may be used in hedges or as specimen shrubs and need no regular pruning. The evergreen and variegated species may be grown against walls (*E. fortunei*), in containers or as ground cover, while *E. japonicus* makes a neat, slow growing evergreen hedge. Trim hedges once or twice during summer, the other evergreens need no regular pruning.

New plants of evergreen species may be raised from cuttings rooted in a cold frame. Deciduous kinds may be grown from seed.

Arranging

This genus includes the spindle berry *E. europaeus*, which I can remember as a child when helping my mother with her arrangements by hunting for this along the roadside. What a treasure it is when you find a well berried bush. It can be used to brighten up dried groups or mixed with flowers in shades of pink. The variegated evergreen euonymus species give interest when added to winter vases.

Preparation

Hammer stem ends and give a long warm drink.

Euphorbia

characias	1 m
cyparissias	25 cm
dulcis	30 cm
griffithii 'Fireglow'	75 cm
lathyrus	1 m
marginata	60 cm
myrsinites	15 cm
niciciana	60 cm
polychroma (epithymoides)	45 cm
robbiae	50 cm
wulfenii	90 cm

Accommodating as to soil, these euphorbias bring a glow of colour from flowers or foliage into any garden. *E. lathyrus*, in addition to being a handsome biennial, is reputed to make soil unattractive to moles, possibly from a taint left where it has grown. It sets seed freely once established. *E. polychroma* is quite a spring tonic with bright yellow flower heads, while *E. dulcis* is at its best in autumn with rich colouring.

Seed may be sown in spring outdoors and most species divide readily after flowering. Cuttings from the base may also be taken and rooted in a cold frame.

1   *Echinops ritro*
2   *Achillea filipendulina* 'Gold Plate'

E. cyparissias tends to be invasive unless kept on poor, dry soil. The milky juice in stems may cause skin irritation and is known to be an irritant poison to human beings and animals.

Arranging
I think this genus provides some of the most striking green material to use in any green arrangements. The species also flower over a long period and have good winter foliage. *E. dulcis* and *E. g.* 'Fireglow' produce effective autumn colours to arrange with bronze and red flowers and berries.

Preparation
Beware of the poisonous milky fluid exuded and dip stem ends in boiling water as soon as possible after cutting. Then give a really long drink.

Euphorbia characias

Filipendula

| ulmaria 'Aurea' | 50 cm |
| hexapetala 'Flore Pleno' *(Spiraea filipendula)* | 60 cm |

Good, deep, really moist loams suit these dainty cream flowered plants best. The leaves are attractive all through the season and enhance the flower heads when these open in summer.
Plants divide readily in early spring.

Arranging
This is a good plant which produces effective foliage as well as flowers. The blooms are most useful when arranged with other delicate material and the golden variegated foliage of *F. ulmaria* 'Aurea' is lovely when mixed with yellow flowers.

Preparation
Hammer stem ends and place in warm water.

Filipendula ulmaria 'Aurea'

Forsythia

x *intermedia* 'Lynwood'	AGM	2 m
intermedia 'Spectabilis'	AGM	2 m
suspensa fortunei		2 – 3 m

Barely 150 years ago, golden forsythia was just introduced to Britain from China and Japan. Now so much a part of our spring gardens we can hardly believe the plant is not a native. Forsythia thrives in most soils and *F. suspensa fortunei* is well adapted to training against a wall.
Prune out some older, darker wood each year as the flowers fade.

Propagation is easy from hard wood cuttings of firm young shoots in autumn, outdoors. Low branches may also be tip-layered.

If birds are troublesome, destroying the flower buds, cast some strands of black cotton across the bush.

Arranging

The first breath of spring! Cut some buddy branches from the garden and bring them into the warm and you will have at least a month's pleasure from the golden flowers. You can also arrange this shrub with the first daffodils.

Preparation

Hammer stem ends well and place in warm water. If forcing, give fresh warm water daily.

Forsythia

Galanthus

nivalis	15 cm
nivalis 'Flore-Pleno'	15 cm
elwesii	20 cm

The common snowdrop and its double form, both so welcome in early spring, grow happily in filtered shade under trees, in open grassy sites or cultivated borders. *G. elwesii* needs full sun. It flowers rather later in the season.

Plant bulbs 5 – 6 cm deep and 3 – 4 cm apart in autumn to begin with. Once clumps are established, lift and divide them as soon as the flowers die down. That way, each new clump will multiply throughout the summer and be as full of blossom as ever the next spring. Never allow the bulbs to get dry.

Seeds may be sown in spring to produce flowering bulbs in three years.

Arranging

Snowdrops, both double and single, are most effective if used as part of a miniature spring garden in a dish or on a slab of wood.

Preparation

A diagonal cut and a good drink.

Galtonia candicans

Galtonia

candicans   1·2 m

This summer flowering bulb comes to us from South Africa. It is perhaps the hardiest species for this country and should first be set in spring 12 cm deep and not subsequently disturbed. A site in full sun on the border is most suitable.

If bulbs are divided, offsets may be carefully removed for replanting. Seed may be sown in spring in a cold frame and will produce flowering bulbs in four or five years.

Arranging

Having such dainty white hanging bells on long firm stems, galtonia is a perfect flower to add to wedding pedestal arrangements.

Preparation

A diagonal cut and a long drink.

Garrya elliptica

Garrya

elliptica   AGM (male form)   1 – 2 m

This has become a very popular evergreen for a

specimen bush or as a wall shrub, growing on a wide range of soils. The male form has long, grey-green catkins in early spring, but the female bushes are also charming with their deep brownish-purple fruits in autumn.

Little pruning is required except where wall or fence trained bushes exceed their space, when long shoots may be cut out after flowering.

Seed may be sown in pans in a cold frame in September, or half ripened wood cuttings may be taken in summer. Layers may also root if pegged down in September.

Arranging

Sprays of the beautiful grey-green catkins are among the most useful subjects for inclusion in many winter arrangements. Before the spring flowers become available this shrub can just be used with other greenery, as the interest is again provided by the contrasting and durable catkins.

Preparation

Hammer stem ends and give a long drink. Preserve by glycerine method.

Gladiolus nanus colvillei

Gladiolus

nanus colvillei varieties	50 cm
primulinus hybrids including Butterfly types	80 cm

Gladioli grow from corms, none of which are fully hardy in Britain. The original species came from warmer parts in south and central Africa. Corms of *G. nanus* varieties are usually grown in very cool conditions under glass. They are set in autumn five to a 15 cm pot of light, rich compost and will flower in spring. In very sheltered areas the corms may be set on well drained borders outdoors, 8 cm deep and 15 cm apart.
Corms of the *G. primulinus* hybrids are larger and may be set outdoors in spring 10 cm deep and 15 cm apart.
Stake the flower spikes in good time and lift the corms in autumn except in really warm areas. The tiny cormels saved from the sides of the large corms may be grown on to flowering size.
We have not listed large flowered types as we consider these smaller selections to be infinitely more attractive for arrangements.

Arranging

With colour shades ranging from white to pink, salmon, and red, the taller stemmed *G. primulinus* hybrids are grand for large church or house groups. The *G. n. colvillei* types, being shorter and more slender are a joy to use in many less ambitious arrangements as they give such a graceful outline. Pick off the flowers as they die.

Preparation

Cut the stem diagonally as the first flower opens and give a really long drink.

Gypsophila

paniculata 'Bristol Fairy'	AGM	90 cm
paniculata 'Flamingo'		90 cm

These dainty double flowers, borne so profusely in summer, are two of the best loved perennial varieties. They will thrive in any well drained, good soil but do often need replacing after a life of three or four years. The pink variety 'Flamingo', is rather less hardy than the white. Flowering stems should be cut off promptly when blossom is over.
It is possible to take soft cuttings from basal shoots in summer and to root these in a cold frame. They should stay in the frame until the following spring before being planted out.

Arranging

These delicate flowers are a must for wedding arrangements. I also like to break the stems down and use them in candelabras for special occasions.

Preparation

Lightly hammer stem ends and give a good drink. To preserve, hang stems upside down to dry.

Gypsophila paniculata (centre)

Hebe

armstrongii	80 cm
'Autumn Glory' AGM	50 cm
brachysiphon (traversii)	1·6 m
'Great Orme' AGM	1 m
hulkeana	1·5 m
'Marjorie'	1 m
rakaiensis (subalpina)	60 cm

Attractive evergreen foliage is an added bonus to this genus of dainty, summer flowering shrubs. Formerly known as shrubby veronicas, they will thrive on almost any well drained soil except in the very coldest areas. Particularly good near the sea where the foliage seems able to withstand the salt laden breezes, they also adapt to town gardens.
Of neat habit, they need no regular pruning, but if

frost damage occurs, bushes will often break again from the base if pruned hard back to just above ground level in April.

Half ripened wood cuttings set in a cold frame in summer are usually successful.

Arranging
If you grow a selection of these lovely evergreen shrubs you should never be without leafy material. I find this neat foliage will always make a background, while flowering stems can be introduced into summer and autumn arrangements, adding light touches of white and mauve.

Preparation
Hammer or split stem ends.

Hebe 'Great Orme'

Hedera

canariensis 'Gloire de Marengo'	3 – 4 m
colchica 'Dentata' AGM	3 m
helix 'Buttercup'	1·2 m
helix 'Cristata'	2 m
helix 'Glacier'	2 m
helix 'Goldheart'	1·5 m
helix 'Hibernica'	2 m
helix 'Sagittifolia'	2 m
helix 'Silver Queen'	2 m

The ivies are such valuable plants for ground or wall cover and for decoration at all seasons of the year that nurserymen are now offering an increasing selection.

Any soil, aspect or situation seems to suit the majority, 'Gloire de Marengo' being the least hardy, welcomes a sheltered corner.

We use them, along with climbing roses, to clothe a pergola (attracting a wide range of birds to nest there) and a plant of 'Goldheart' scrambles happily through the lower branches of *Prunus cerasifera* 'Pissardii'. Another plant of 'Goldheart', set in an earthenware container, and top dressed periodically, climbs the wall to peep in at the kitchen window.

Ivies may be pruned back in April and again later in the season if necessary.

Propagation is by cutting or rooted layers.

Arranging
This most useful material provides trailing branches in such a splendid variety of colours. It is wonderful for giving a flowing look to the base of arrangements.

Preparation
Hammer or split stem ends. Berried sprays can be preserved with glycerine.

Hedera colchica 'Dentata'

Helenium

autumnale	1 – 1·5 m

This species came originally from North America and today there is a wide range of herbaceous varieties which extend the season from June to September. Colours vary from the original yellow to bronze and warm browns. All have the characteristic cone-shaped centres.

If the first flower stem is shortened several weeks before buds open, branching stems will often develop. All heleniums have stout stems and seldom need staking. They thrive in any good soil and prefer sunny borders.

Arranging
These bright flowers last well and look good in mixed vases.

Preparation
Hammer stem ends and give a warm drink.

A hybrid helenium

Helichrysum

angustifolium		60 cm
plicatum		60 cm
splendidum		60 cm
bracteatum mixed	annual	30 cm
monstrosum mixed		60 cm

Although the flowers of perennial helichrysums are of little value, the grey and silver leaves are an asset to any border. Only provide the plants with dry conditions, full sunlight and well drained soil. *H. angustifolium* is one of the most reliable, being always bright silver. *H. splendidum* is perhaps the hardiest of this grey selection.

Heeled cuttings taken in July or August will root in cold frame or gentle heat.

Both short and tall annual varieties may be sown in heat in March or direct on a warm outdoor border in April or May to flower from July until the autumn.

Arranging
The annual varieties are mainly used for brightening up dried winter arrangements but the heads look very effective individually pinned to a cone of Styrofoam. The grey and silver foliage of the other varieties combines well with dainty pink and white flowers.

Preparation
Strip off the leaves of the annual varieties and hang upside down to dry. To use them on stems, push a florist's wire through the flower centre and down the stem before drying. With the grey and silver perennials, lightly hammer stem ends and give a good drink.

Helichrysum angustifolium

Helleborus

foetidus	60 cm
lividus corsicus AGM	60 cm
niger AGM	40 cm
orientalis AGM	50 cm

Shade at the roots, good moist soil and ample organic matter will suit all these species. They will grow on soils where chalk is present if the other provisions are supplied. Good growth of healthy foliage will provide the shade needed for the rather fleshy roots.

Plants dislike being moved, but with care they can be divided and replanted before they become dry. We find our plants seed very readily.

All parts of each of the species, even the beautiful Christmas rose are poisonous to man and animal.

Arranging

The white flowers of *H. niger* are such a beautiful addition to the fresh Christmas table arrangement. The other helleborus species, in shades of green, pink and purple, are a must for the arranger because they are among the few plants to bloom in early spring and look most effective with the many bulbous flowers which come along at the same season.

Preparation

Hammer stem ends and dip in boiling water for a few minutes, then stand them in deep water at least overnight.

Heuchera

'Bressingham Hybrids'	75 – 90 cm
sanguinea 'Greenfinch'	75 cm
x *Heucherella tiarelloides*	30 cm

These interesting hybrids, with handsome mounds of foliage and dainty flower spikes thrive in any well drained soil. They will also grow in light shade, and given these conditions will continue to flower throughout the summer.

It is best to divide the roots every three years, planting the younger crowns deeply and firmly in freshly prepared soil after the flowering period.

Many modern hybrids in a wide variety of pink, coral and crimson shades, as well as those with sulphur yellow spikes like *H. s.* 'Greenfinch' have originated from Blooms Nurseries at Bressingham in Norfolk.

Arranging

Varieties from this genus are an absolute must for any flower arranger. The slender stems, bearing petite bells, add grace to any summer arrangement. The evergreen leaves can be used as a base for quite small arrangements all the year round.

Preparation

A diagonal cut and a long drink. The leaves benefit from their ends being dipped in boiling water and then being completely submerged in cold water for several hours.

Heuchera, a most useful plant for foliage and flower

Hippophae

rhamnoides	3 m

The sea buckthorn with slender grey-green leaves and gay orange berries in autumn makes a splendid hedge or wind-break. The bushes should be set 70 cm apart in groups to ensure cross pollination for berry production as male and female flowers are borne on separate bushes.

Once established, these twiggy shrubs grow rapidly giving protection against wind or interlopers and providing a pleasing background for more tender genera.

Little pruning is necessary except to keep bushes within their prescribed area.

Seed may be stratified in autumn. Shoots may be layered, or root cuttings taken, in early spring.

Arranging
This species is mainly used for the long stems of orange berries which last well into the winter and add colour to any dried arrangement.

Preparation
Hammer stem ends and give a long drink. The berries dry off on the stems in water though they shrivel slightly.

Hosta

albomarginata	50 cm
crispula AGM	50 cm
fortunei 'Albopicta' AGM	60 cm
fortunei 'Aurea'	50 cm
fortunei 'Aureomarginata'	65 cm
'Frances Williams'	1 m
sieboldiana AGM	60 cm
sieboldiana 'Elegans' AGM	60 cm
tardiana	40 cm
'Thomas Hogg'	60 cm
undulata 'Medio-Variegata'	35 cm

There is a wealth of choice in this genus of plantain lilies. They are such dual purpose plants with vari-egated or waved leaves and slender spikes of white or lilac flowers in summer. Even the seed heads have their own charm.

They need deep, moisture-retentive soil and do not dislike shade. They will thrive near the edge of pond or stream. To keep plants growing well, top dress round the crowns each year, with well rotted compost. The roots are tough subjects but can be divided in spring. Seed sown in spring indoors germinates readily but if cross pollination has taken place, seedlings may not come true to type.

Arranging
This genus provides the most valuable asset to any flower arranger's garden. The variety of leaves produced by the species mentioned above will give you a never ending supply of wonderful material for all types of arrangements including all-green compositions.

Preparation
Submerge the leaves in cold water for several hours. The seed heads can be preserved by picking just as they are starting to dry on the plant and then hanging them upside down indoors. The leaves can be pressed.

Hostas are invaluable for flower arranging, providing a range of leaf colour and texture

Humulus

lupulus 'Aureus'   4 m
japonicus 'Variegatus'   3 m

The golden and silver-leafed forms of hop plants colour best in a sunny site. They need good, deep soil and will cover unsightly walls or buildings very happily. Seed of both perennial and annual species may be sown indoors in March or on sites outdoors in May. The perennial hop *H. l.* 'Aureus', may be divided in early spring. The long bines made during summer should be cut off in autumn.

The flower heads (really the hop fruits) are green at first, later turning a russet brown.

Arranging

This is excellent material for providing long trails which give a flowing line to large arrangements. The leaves can also be used on their own as a base for groups in smaller containers.

Preparation

Lightly hammer or split stem ends and give a long drink. Flowers can be dried by hanging stems upside down.

Hypericum

androsaemum   1 m
calycinum   30 cm
'Hidcote'   AGM   1·2 m

These gay, adaptable shrubs thrive in any soil or site, dry, sunny or shady.

H. calycinum, the dwarf evergreen rose of Sharon with golden flowers open throughout the summer, is excellent for covering dry banks with neat matted growth. Use shears to cut back the old shoots each spring.

H. 'Hidcote' is a superb, cheerful shrub for large or small gardens, its rich gold blossoms are open from July until October. Prune older stems out to the base in early spring.

These species may be increased by division and *H. androsaemum* also by stratified berries.

Arranging

This is a genus which provides the arranger with three types of material, the evergreen foliage, the yellow flowers and the berried sprays. I usually use the sprays cut short in small arrangements.

Preparation

Lightly hammer or split stem ends and give a good drink.

Hypericum 'Hidcote'

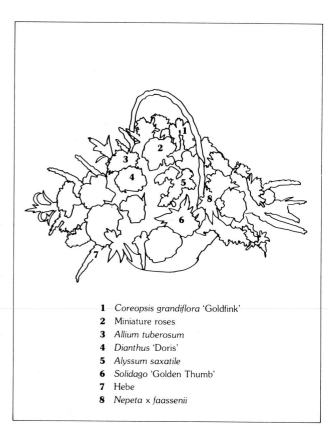

1 *Coreopsis grandiflora* 'Goldfink'
2 Miniature roses
3 *Allium tuberosum*
4 *Dianthus* 'Doris'
5 *Alyssum saxatile*
6 *Solidago* 'Golden Thumb'
7 Hebe
8 *Nepeta* x *faassenii*

Hyssopus

officinale   30 – 50 cm

Centuries ago this hardy little evergreen herb came to us from southern Europe. The narrow leaves are aromatic and the flowers a brilliant blue. It grows most happily in light soil on warm, sunny borders either among other herbs or with the herbaceous flowers.
Cut back straggly shoots in April.
Seed may be sown outdoors in spring or cuttings will root in a cold frame during the summer.

Arranging
This is another flower very suitable for cottage-type arrangements of mixed summer flowers as it has a rather informal habit of growth.

Preparation
A diagonal cut and a good drink. Dry seed heads by hanging them upside down.

Iberis umbellata, a hardy annual

Iberis

commutatum	15 cm
umbellata	30 cm

In this genus of candytufts we have chosen a prostrate evergreen *I. commutatum* which shines with brilliant white flower heads from May to July, and the hardy annual species with pink, white and mauve varieties, *I. umbellata*.
Either is suitable for the edge of a container or border, for a patch on the rock garden or a crevice in the patio.
Seed of annual kinds may be sown direct outdoors in any sunny area in spring. The perennial is sown in April in a cold frame and cuttings of established plants are easy to take during summer. Perennial roots also divide in early spring.

Arranging
This is a pretty little flower in pastel shades suitable for small arrangements either on its own or blended with other small summer flowers.

Preparation
A diagonal cut and a good drink. Dry, when flowers have run to seed, by hanging them upside down.

Ilex

aquifolium 'J.C. van Tol'	AGM	2 m
aquifolium 'Silver Queen'	AGM	2 m
x *altaclarensis* 'Golden King'	AGM	2 m

It is always a little misleading to find that holly 'Silver Queen' bears no fruit whereas 'Golden King' berries well. However, both are lovely for their variegated evergreen foliage and along with the third variety 'J.C. van Tol', which also berries well, they make fine specimen bushes or stout hedges and wind-breaks. 'Golden King' and 'J.C. van Tol' are almost spineless. They seem to grow in almost any soil and situation, only disliking the tops of dry banks. September and April are the best planting months. Small bushes transplant best, and if not container grown, nursery-men often ball the roots in sacking for customers, as holly dislikes disturbance.
Prune with secateurs to remove straggling shoots in April.
Seed may be stratified in autumn for green varieties but variegated forms are grafted. Hollies are not easy from cuttings.

Arranging
I think everyone has their favourite way of using holly

at Christmas. I like to use it in a dish with Oasis and place a red candle in the centre. An all round arrangement with holly and nine Christmas roses, which could be the artificial type, is another attractive theme.

Preparation
Holly lasts better in damp Oasis than in water and benefits from being sprayed with a clear varnish. If you need to use it in water, then split the stem ends.

look. It makes a striking addition to an arrangement of blue-pink blooms and the glossy leaves are very useful to outline groups of flowers in medium sized vases.

Preparation
A diagonal cut and a good drink.

Incarvillea delavayi

Incarvillea

delavayi AGM	45 cm

About a century ago this lovely herbaceous perennial was brought over from China. It is unique among hardy plants in its deep pink, trumpet shaped flowers which open in June and July.

It needs a sunny, sheltered border on rich, well drained soil. The crowns, which die right back from autumn until April, should be covered by dry litter during the winter.

Seed may be sown in spring, the seedlings taking two years to reach flowering size. Plants are best transplanted while dormant.

Arranging
This is an unusual flower which has rather a tropical

Iris pallida 'Aurea Variegata'

Iris

danfordiae	10 cm
histrioides	10 cm
reticulata	15 cm
chrysographes 'Black Velvet'	60 cm
foetidissima 'Citrina'	60 cm
foetidissima 'Variegata' AGM	50 cm
kaempferi	75 cm
sibirica 'Alba'	75 cm
germanica	1 m
pallida 'Aurea Variegata'	60 cm
pseudacorus 'Variegata'	1 m
unguicularis (stylosa) AGM	15 cm

This is such a wide ranging genus that we have grouped the species according to their site requirements.

Those in group one are tiny, early flowering bulbous species suitable for growing in deep pans in a cold conservatory, in containers to brighten the patio, or in groups on the rock garden among other small, early bulbs. They are planted in autumn.

The species in group two enjoy moist soil and will grow in rather shady areas. They are taller and flower in summer. The rootstocks can be divided.

Group three includes the precious winter flowering *I. unguicularis* from Algeria which loves dry soil under shelter of a south facing wall, and the huge group of varieties of *I. germanica* whose flowers in so many wonderful shades, grace our borders in June. They all ask for shallow planting in sunny well drained alkaline soil. The variegated forms listed are chosen for the interesting colours of their foliage which is retained throughout the year. This group may also be increased by division.

Arranging

How lucky we are to have such a wide variety of colours and shapes in the iris genus. I sometimes make a line arrangement with five iris on a plate with some hosta leaves at the base, and I like the flag varieties in big mixed summer vases. The little spring species look rather nice in a small cut glass vase.

Preparation

A diagonal cut and then give a long drink.

Jasminum

nudiflorum	AGM	3 – 4 m
officinale 'Affine'		6 – 8 m

This is another genus, which, introduced from the Far East, has made itself very much at home here thriving in most soils and situations. *J. o.* 'Affine' needs a sheltered corner if grown in the north of England. Both, if supported, will cover large areas of wall.

J. nudiflorum flowers with golden stars on bare green stems in mid-winter. It may be trained over a building or allowed to make a flowering mound. Long shoots can be pruned back after flowering. If the plant becomes a thicket, hard pruning into old wood will rejuvenate and control the size. This species often tip roots where arching shoots touch the ground.

J. officinale, the fragrant white summer species, grows from seed of berries scattered by birds. It may also be layered.

Both can be increased from hard wood cuttings in autumn.

Arranging

I use short pieces of *J. nudiflorum* with the first small spring flowers of the year. *J. officinale* produces such

sweetly scented white flowers on flowing branches that it is perfect for coming over the edge of pedestals in summer. Its evergreen foliage is useful for much of the year.

Preparation

Dip stem ends in boiling water then give a good long cold drink.

Juniperus sabina tamariscifolia

Juniperus

sabina tamariscifolia	AGM	60 cm
prostrate, spreading to 1·5 m		
squamata 'Meyeri' up to		1·3 m
spreading to 1·5 m		

Once established, these spreading, low growing junipers not only enhance garden borders, but may usefully screen man-hole covers, clothe dry banks, or deck the edge of terrace or patio with attractive evergreen foliage.

By their habit of low growth, these conifers need no regular pruning but any branches which outgrow their allotted space, may always be selected for cutting for arrangements.

J. sabina tamariscifolia is the more prostrate species,

the grey-green branches growing layer on layer and making excellent ground cover.

J. squamata 'Meyeri' is a beautiful blue green with arching, spreading branches which make dense ground cover to the area over which they extend.

Junipers are best transplanted in early autumn or late spring and seem happy on any well drained site.

Please refer to the chapter on cultural hints for note on spraying evergreens.

They may be increased by heeled, hard wood cuttings set in a cold frame or outdoors in the autumn.

Arranging

A very good all round foliage which is available the entire year. I tend to use this material in medium sized arrangements and the blue variety looks most effective with similarly coloured or white flowers.

Preparation

Hammer or split stem ends and give a good drink.

Kerria

japonica 'Pleniflora'	AGM	1·8 m
japonica 'Variegata' ('Picta')		1·3 m

Kerria japonica 'Pleniflora'

Kerria is a real cottage garden favourite, its double orange-yellow flowers, on bright green stems, may often be seen beside garden gate or arching over the cottage door. The variegated form is equally dainty and rather lower growing.

Old shoots may be cut right out after flowering and brown tips cut back to green wood in early spring.

Both shrubs sucker freely and are easy to divide.

Arranging

As kerria can be cut on long stems, it is invaluable for making a good background to daffodils and other spring flowers which are cut without their foliage. The yellow button-like flowers give added interest.

Preparation

Hammer stem ends and give a long drink.

Kniphofia

'Green Jade'		1·2 m
'Little Maid'		60 cm
'Maid of Orleans'	AGM	1·2 m

A yellow form of kniphofia

Among the many hybrid red hot poker varieties available today, we have suggested three with rather delicate colours, as their names suggest.

These herbaceous plants are not always easy, especially on heavy soils, and, coming originally from the warmer parts of Africa, very much dislike the damp cold of our English winters.

Light, well drained soil and a sunny aspect are essential. For smaller gardens, the shorter varieties are perhaps the best to grow. Set the plants in spring, taking care never to let the fleshy roots dry.

Established crowns can be divided in spring just after growth has begun, again keeping the roots from drying. Seed will germinate but usually does not come true to type.

Arranging

Because of their spiky habit, kniphofias are among the most valuable summer flowers to give height to mixed arrangements. They also break up any flatness which may result from the introduction of daisy type flowers of which there is such a wide selection at this season.

Preparation

A diagonal cut and a good long drink.

Lathyrus

latifolius	2·5 m
odoratus	2 m
rotundifolius	1·5 m

Annual sweet peas, *L. odoratus* need no introduction: there is a wide choice of varieties. If you choose to grow plants without staking, select dwarf growing strains from the catalogue, for the colours are as vivid and varied as those of the tall growing cultivars. Sow the seed in pots in spring (or autumn) and harden off in a cold frame before planting into well prepared ground in April.

The two other perennial species are hardy and will scramble over fence or hedge. They provide a steady supply of smaller pink, red or mauve flowers throughout the summer.

These too, may be raised from seed in spring.

Arranging

I think the delicately shaded sweet peas are shown to advantage when arranged in a container which complements their daintiness and colour. I like to use a shell or a white porcelain vase and group them with some kind of feathery grey foliage.

Preparation

Gather before the top flower has opened and give the stems a diagonal cut and a deep drink. Avoid laying the stems down too much because of bruising the blossoms.

Lavandula spica 'Hidcote'

Lavandula

spica		1 m
spica 'Hidcote'	AGM	30 cm
vera		60 cm

Of all fragrant herbs, lavender is the best beloved. It grows so well in sunny, well drained soils and both grey foliage and flowers are scented.

It makes charming low hedges, the smaller species excel as an edging to rose beds and specimen plants will add character to a patio or the front of a shrub border.

Cut off flower stems in autumn and prune back straggly branches hard in April.

Hard wood heeled cuttings may be rooted outdoors in autumn.

Arranging

I always enjoy using lavandula mixed with pink or pale mauve flowers in the summer. Its spiky habit gives an attractive outline and as a bonus it fills the room with a wonderful fragrance. Its longevity in water is an added advantage.

Preparation

Just cut the stems and place in water; they will even dry off in a vase. If you want to keep the seeds for pot pourri etc., then gather when the flowers are fully open, bunch together and hang them upside down in a warm place.

Both increase freely in dampish, shady areas and may be naturalised in grass along with other spring flowering bulbs.

L. aestivum, a native of England, has more flowers to a stem than the early flowering *L. vernum.*

Set the bulbs 9 cm deep in autumn. They may not bloom the first year but once established will flower freely and seldom need to be disturbed.

Arranging

This is a very useful flower which, from its dainty shape, earns the nickname of snowflake. I enjoy using *L. vernum* when the snowdrops are over. *L. aestivum* comes even later providing pure white heads, tipped green, to mix in with the late spring flowers.

Preparation

A diagonal cut and a long drink.

Leucojum aestivum

Leucojum

aestivum	50 cm
vernum	20 cm

These spring snowflakes follow our snowdrops to provide drooping heads of white and green flowers from February to May.

Leycesteria formosa

Leycesteria

formosa   1·3 m

This is an unusual shrub from the Himalayas. The stems, rather like green bamboos, bear heavy leaves and are topped in summer with drooping racemes of dark red bracts and white flowers. The bracts remain around the shiny purple berries which follow.

The bush seems to grow happily in most soils. Stems may be thinned out to ground level in early spring. Propagation is easy from stratified berries.

Arranging
What a talking point you create by using pieces of this very unusual shrub. Either in its flowering or berried form it looks most effective when introduced into a vase of mauves and purples.

Preparation
Strip off 3 – 5 cm of the bark, split stem ends and then give a good long drink. Remove some of the foliage to reveal the beautiful white flowers and crimson bracts.

Liatris

callilepis 'Kobold'   70 cm
pycnostachya   80 cm – 1 m
spicata   50 cm

These gay purple herbaceous perennials from North America need well drained, light soil in a sunny site. All three species have a rather upright habit and flower from July to September.

The tuberous roots may be divided in spring or plants may be raised from seed sown outdoors in early summer.

Arranging
Because of its late summer flowering habit, this is very useful tall spiky material to add to large mixed vases. At this period there is a glut of flat headed flowers which particularly need contrasting shapes arranged with them.

Preparation
Strip off lower leaves and hammer stem ends, then give a long drink.

Liatris spicata

Ligularia stenocephala

Ligularia

dentata 'Desdemona'	AGM	1 m
stenocephala		1·2 m

These are handsome plants for damp soils near the waterside where their majestic branching stems of orange daisies catch the eye in late summer and autumn.

Plants can be divided in spring.

Arranging

I always feel these stately flowers should be arranged so that the black stems can be seen and admired, therefore a line arrangement, using their own large leaves at the base, is the way to use them to best advantage.

Preparation

Hammer stem ends and give a long drink.

Ligustrum ovalifolium 'Aureum'

Ligustrum

lucidum 'Golden Wax'	2 m
ovalifolium 'Aureum'	1·2 m
vulgare	1·5 m

The ubiquitous privet, in its coloured forms has much to commend it to the flower arranger. Almost evergreen, fast growing and tolerant of most soils and situations, it colours best in sunny sites. The leaves of L. l. 'Golden Wax' are particularly thick. Planting time is September or April.

The bushes may be left to grow naturally or trimmed as a hedge once or twice during the growing season. Hard wood cuttings root readily outdoors in autumn. L. vulgare produces black berries which may be stratified.

Arranging

This is a long lasting foliage which, being evergreen, provides the arranger with background material all the year round. The flowers are rarely used because of the fact that privet is so often grown as hedging and therefore clipped before the flowering season. If grown as a bush, then do use the flowers of L. vulgare.

Preparation

Hammer or split stem ends and give a good long drink.

Lilium

auratum	1·2 m
candidum (Madonna lily)	1·2 m
x hollandicum (umbellatum)	80 cm
martagon	90 cm
regale	1·5 m
x testaceum	1·5 m

From this genus, with a never ending supply of fine, new hybrids, we have selected six well tried species.

They all need well drained land and in heavy clay soil, special raised beds incorporating coarse sand and good rotted compost should be prepared. On the other hand, the bulbs must never dry out. Cool conditions at the edge of a shrubbery, where the flowers can still open in sunlight, are ideal. Peat or leaf-mould should be mixed into the soil before planting.

Stem rooting species as L. auratum and L. regale, are helped if the stems are earthed up a little as they grow. L. auratum dislikes lime in soil, the other five species are lime tolerant.

The flowering season with these six species extends from May to late July. It is wise to give a liquid feed at flowering time to help build up the bulbs for the next year.

L. candidum may be transplanted, when this is necessary, just after flowering. All the other species are best replanted in early spring. Never let the bulbs dry while out of the soil.

Some species seldom set seed and *L. martagon* is very slow to reach flowering stage from seed. By contrast, *L. regale* is very quick, flowering two years from seed sowing. Plants raised from seed are free from virus diseases to start with. Vegetative methods are liable to spread disease if propagating material is taken from infected bulbs.

Lily species and varieties look best in the garden in groups of one variety rather than in mixed plantings. For the patio or cold conservatory, *L. auratum, L. candidum* and *L. regale* may be grown in tubs or large pots. Bulbs are set half way down the pots in light compost and top dressed as they grow until the pots are full. If left in the pots for subsequent years remove the top 12 cm of the compost and replace with new enriched supplies.

Arranging
What a beautiful genus of flowers. As they are so regal I honestly prefer to arrange a few specimens on their own, using no other foliage than that of the lilies.

Preparation
A diagonal cut and place in warm water for a few hours, then give a long cold drink. Seed heads can be dried when green, by standing stems in 5 cm of water in a warm dry atmosphere.

Limonium latifolium

Limonium

incanum (Statice incanum)	15 cm
latifolium (Statice latifolium)	65 cm

These useful perennial statice plants are attractive in summer, *L. latifolium* in particular, with its many finely branched stems of tiny, lavender coloured flowers. Both are specially valuable when dried for long lasting winter decoration.

Grow them both in well drained, open, sunny sites and they should be long lived.

Both may be raised from seed sown in April. Division is possible but not easy.

Arranging
These plants are an absolute gift to the enthusiast for dried winter decorations as they brighten up the browns of dried material. I use tiny pieces to put in miniature shell arrangements.

Preparation
A diagonal cut and a good drink. Dry by hanging them upside down.

Lilies, massed together for maximum impact

Lonicera nitida 'Baggesen's Gold' and sedum (left)

Lonicera

fragrantissima	1·3 m
nitida 'Baggesen's Gold'	1 m
x *purpusii*	1·2 m
japonica 'Aureoreticulata' AGM	3 m
japonica 'Halliana' AGM	4 m
periclymenum 'Belgica' ('Early Dutch')	4 m
x *tellmanniana* AGM	4 m
tragophylla	4 m

Honeysuckle flowers are old favourites. With this selection, it is almost possible to have one species in bloom all the year round.

L. fragrantissima and *L.* x *purpusii* are bush species flowering from November to March. Along with the other bush type *L. n.* 'Baggesen's Gold', grown mainly for its foliage, they need full sunlight and good rich soil. Pruning is to thin out the older wood after flowering.

The five climbing species listed next need their roots in shade and in good moist soil. With their natural twining habit, they are better suited to growing through an old tree or over a stump than to training on a house wall. *L. tragophylla* will only thrive in complete shade while the hybrid *L.* x *tellmanniana* will not succeed in north or east facing aspects. The flowering season extends from late May to October. Nothing leads to sudden attacks of aphis more quickly than to have a honeysuckle in too dry a site.

These plants may be rooted from soft cuttings indoors, hard wood cuttings outdoors, or from stratified seed.

Prune the climbing species by cutting out old flowered wood and if training the plants, tying in strong new shoots.

L. j. 'Halliana' is so vigorous, once it settles down, it may need cutting back several times during the late summer, but its long season of fragrant flowers justifies all the effort.

Arranging
We are lucky to have such a wonderful selection of species from this genus. I always mentally associate honeysuckle with a rustic setting, so often arrange the sweet scented varieties in a basket or wooden container. If you have a gnarled-looking piece of driftwood, this can well be incorporated into an arrangement of lonicera. For variegation, or whenever light foliage is required, use *L. nitida* 'Baggesen's Gold'.

Preparation
Hammer or split stem ends and give a long deep drink.

Lunaria

annua (biennis) mixed	80 cm
annua 'Variegata'	1 m

The well known purple flowered honesty is easy to grow from seed sown in spring on a shady site, either where it is to bloom, or on a seed bed for transplanting later among shrubs or below a hedge. It will flower in May the following year. Seed heads are ready to gather in August.

Arranging
This plant is very rarely used in its flowering form but nearly always when dried. The silvery seed pods can look most striking arranged on their own against a very dark background.

Preparation
Dip flower stem ends in boiling water then give a long drink. To preserve, hang stems upside down to dry as soon as the seed has formed. To obtain the silvery 'pennies' gently rub off outer casings between finger and thumb.

Lupinus

arboreus	1 – 1·2 m
hartwegii	80 cm
polyphyllus	80 cm – 1 m

Here are three very distinct species.

L. arboreus is a short lived bush thriving in poor dry conditions on banks or sunny slopes. It flowers freely in cream, white and yellow and seeds equally freely in the vicinity.

L. hartwegii is a pretty blue or white flowered annual plant which, if seed is sown outdoors in spring, will flower and complete its life the same year.

L. polyphyllus is the best known kind of lupin with special strains of fine colours selected by skilled plant breeders. These plants are tolerant of any well drained soil except clay. They need neither lime nor manure and thrive in the polluted air of large industrial towns. The plants are perennial but not very long lived and propagation from cuttings of shoots on the fleshy roots is difficult.

Seed therefore, of a good strain, is the best method of renewing stock. Sow seed in spring outdoors to flower in the following year.

Arranging

Although it is difficult to prevent lupins from flagging, I have a special treatment after which I can use them very successfully in big church or marquee groups.

Preparation

This is rather time consuming but worthwhile! Turn flower spike upside down and fill hollow stem with cold water from a jug, then plug the full stem with cottonwool. Seed heads can be preserved by the hanging method.

Lysimachia

ephemerum	1·2 m
nummularia 'Aurea'	10 cm
punctata	90 cm

This is an easy genus, growing well in ordinary soil on any rather moist site. Plants may be divided in spring or raised from seed sown outdoors.

L. nummularia 'Aurea' makes a splendid ground cover in damp areas under bushes. The taller species are both attractive herbaceous plants in damp or waterside gardens.

Arranging

This is not a commonly used plant for flower arranging but I feel it should be given recognition. *L. ephemerum* produces such pretty stems of grey leaves and slender spikes of grey-white flowers which are very effective rising from the base of a large arrangement. *L. nummularia* is useful for the base of pedestals.

Preparation

Lightly hammer stem ends and give a long drink.

Lythrum salicaria

Lythrum

salicaria	1 m
virgatum	80 cm

These species of loosestrife are both in rosy purple shades and each flowers between July and September. Both are long lived species, thriving as in the wild, on damp soils near the waterside, although they will also grow in a herbaceous border.

The rootstock is woody, but cuttings of young shoots may be taken in spring and rooted in a cold frame. Seeds may be sown but the subsequent plants are variable in colour.

Arranging

This is another late summer spiky flowered genus

which can be used in large groups to break up any flatness.

Preparation
Dip stem ends in boiling water, then give a long drink.

The fine, large leaves are invaluable for the base of line arrangements.

Preparation
Dip stem ends in boiling water for a few minutes and then give a really long deep drink.

Macleaya cordata

Mahonia aquifolium

Macleaya

cordata (Bocconia)	1·5 m

This stately plant from China, with such shapely leaves and airy flower plumes, is right for the back of a wide border or in the open shade of a wild garden. It needs good deep soil and ample moisture to produce the graceful flowers in August and September.
The roots are fleshy and root cuttings may be taken or stocks can be carefully divided in spring.

Arranging
I always find these ivory plumes so useful to blend into groups with apricot and beige shades where white flowers would look completely out of place.

Mahonia

aquifolium AGM	80 cm
aquifolium 'Atropurpurea'	1 m
japonica	1·5 m
lomariifolia	1·5 m

These evergreen shrubs thrive in any well drained soils including those over chalk. They will also grow in filtered shade, in fact *M. japonica* welcomes protection afforded by surrounding shrubs to reduce the damage from frost on its flower spikes. *M. lomariifolia*, a very handsome, erect species is only hardy enough to grow in the south of England.
All species have sweetly scented racemes of creamy yellow flowers in mild winters and in early spring. *M. aquifolium* and varieties are rather less spiny than the

other holly leafed species in this genus and they have very glossy foliage. The *M. aquifolium* 'Atropurpureum' is handsomely tinted warm brownish purple throughout most months. The blue berries are beloved by wild birds.

No pruning is needed unless to remove old, dead stems. This should be done in April.

M. aquifolium and its variety, increase readily by suckers and seed may be stratified. The other species can be increased by hard wood cuttings when material is available.

Arranging
Because of its very early flowering habit, sprays of mahonia add charm to any winter arrangement. It is such a pleasure to find a flowering shrub one can use in January vases. The leaves are invaluable all the year round as background material.

Preparation
Either hammer or split stem ends or peel off lower 10 cm of bark and then give a good drink. *M japonica* is a good glycerining subject.

Matthiola bicornis

Matthiola

bicornis	30 cm
incana 'Brompton Hybrids'	30 – 50 cm

Dried up and insignificant by day, but a fragrant joy each summer evening. This describes *M. bicornis*, better known as night-scented stock which opens its starry, four petalled, pink and mauve shaded flowers in the cool hours. We always sow a patch in spring somewhere near a window through which the scent may drift indoors. Any soil and situation is acceptable to this little annual.

M. incana covers a wide range of stouter types of fragrant stocks including the 'Ten Week' and 'Brompton' selections which have been bred to produce fine spikes of double flowers in shades from white through pink to rich purple.

The 'Ten Week' stock is a half hardy annual sown in heat in spring, transplanted to good, sunny outdoor sites in May to flower from June throughout the summer. All stocks are happy in limy soil.

The 'Brompton' stock is a hardy biennial in many areas. Best sown in a cold frame in June and grown on in the frame, with some ventilation, until early spring when the bushy plants are set in the site where they will flower from March to early June. Strains of seed are now available which, if grown in a temperature between 15 – 20°C will show by the seed leaf colour whether they are going to have double or single flowers.

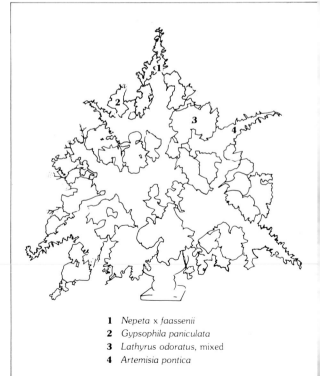

1 *Nepeta* x *faassenii*
2 *Gypsophila paniculata*
3 *Lathyrus odoratus*, mixed
4 *Artemisia pontica*

Arranging

I always think it is vital to grow a couple of rows of stock on a spare piece of ground as these flowers are among the most valuable to the arranger. They can be used in large or small groups, in mixed vases or on their own.

Preparation

Hammer stem ends or dip in boiling water before giving a long cold drink. Be sure to remove all foliage below the water line as the leaves decompose very quickly.

Melissa

| officinalis (balm) | 30 cm |
| officinalis 'Variegata' | 30 cm |

Any sunny or semi-shady site on good garden soil will suit this popular pot herb, which is a herbaceous perennial, making neat clumps of fragrant lemon scented foliage during summer and sprays of small whitish flowers. The variegated and golden forms may be scorched in hot, dry soils.

We always cut the flower spikes off before too much seed is scattered. The seed germinates readily in the open ground in summer.

Arranging

This is not a good lasting material, but if I am desperate for a few variegated stems, I use one or two for a day and then replace.

Preparation

Dip stem ends in boiling water and then give a long drink.

Molucella

| laevis | 50 cm |

Bells of Ireland is not an easy plant to raise. It demands extra care at seed sowing time. Use light, well drained compost and prick out seedlings early into small peat or fibre pots.

Grow the plants on indoors until danger of frost is over, in late May or early June, then transplant, pot and all, without root disturbance, to a sunny well prepared border.

Arranging

This is a lovely subject that looks as good fresh as it

does dried. In its dried form it provides a parchment colour to a mixed dried group.

Preparation

A diagonal cut and give a long cold drink. To dry, remove leaves and hang stems upside down. To obtain dried green specimen, cut while lowest bell is still fresh green.

Molucella laevis

Monarda

| didyma 'Cambridge Scarlet' | 60 – 80 cm |
| didyma 'Croftway Pink' | 60 – 80 cm |

The old fashioned bergamot, with its aromatic leaves, has such unusually shaped blossom heads that every flowering group is of interest. The plants thrive best on good deep soil with ample moisture and grow well in semi-shade. Given the right conditions, the red or pink flowers will continue from June to September. It is herbaceous.

Roots may be readily divided in early spring.

Arranging

I think of these flowers as little mop heads and use them in informal summer arrangements.

Preparation

Dip stem ends in boiling water and then give a long drink.

A form of *Monarda didyma*

Muscari

armeniacum	20 cm
botryoides 'Album'	15 cm
latifolium	30 cm

These little bulbs are very happy naturalised or growing in groups on rock garden or patio. They also flower well in deep pans in a cold conservatory.

The heads of tiny, globular flowers open in spring after the leaves, which often sprout in autumn and withstand the winter.

M. armeniacum is the species most ready to increase either in grass or under spring flowering shrubs. Its flowers are bright blue with a white frilly edge.

M. b. 'Album' is neat and pure white, less vigorous and thus better in rock garden or pans.

M. latifolium, with a much broader leaf, is deep purple blue and less inclined to increase.

All species thrive best in full sun and do not mind lime in soil. Divide the colonies every three or four years.

Arranging

Here is another flower suitable for a moss garden and I love to see them in small mixed spring posies too.

Preparation

A diagonal cut and a good drink. Seed heads can be dried by standing them upright in a little water.

Narcissus

bulbocodium citrinus	10 cm
cyclamineus	15 cm
juncifolius	15 cm
triandrus albus	20 – 25 cm
jonquilla	30 cm
poeticus recurvus (pheasant's eye)	45 cm
'February Gold'	35 cm
'Primrose Cheerfulness'	40 cm

To have seen an alpine meadow covered with the naturalised dwarf species of this genus is an unforgettable experience. In semi-shade, on slightly damp ground, though well drained in summer, these tiny species increase prolifically. They may also be grouped on a rock garden or in deep pans in a cold conservatory.

Plant early, in August or September, 8 cm deep outdoors or in pots, just below the surface. They will flower in early spring.

Of the larger species, *N. jonquilla* with rush-like deep green leaves, has very fragrant heads of small, deep yellow flowers.

The pheasant's eye is the latest to bloom, carrying the season on until late May. White with a deep red eye, it, too is sweetly scented. 'Primrose Cheerfulness' is creamy yellow and fully double, fairly late, with several flowers to a head.

'February Gold' as its name suggests, blooms early. It is a selection from the *N. cyclamineus* group and has dainty reflexed petals. I have often had it flowering among shrubs when there has been snow all around.

The planting season is as for the dwarf species. If bulbs increase readily, there is no need to transplant for several years.

Arranging

Included in this group are the miniature varieties which look very dainty in spring moss gardens. The larger varieties mix well with catkins and can be arranged effectively in a container on a piece of bark with some large green leaves at the base.

Preparation

A diagonal cut and a long deep drink. When gathering from the garden, take a bucket with a little water in the bottom and put the flowers straight into the bucket as you cut them.

Nemesia

strumosa suttoni   30 cm

These are among my favourite annuals for sunny borders, in shades of pink, red, orange, cream and blue. In a dry summer, if regularly deadheaded, they have a long flowering season.
Sow indoors in March, transplant and grow on until late April, then plant 25 cm apart near the front of a border.

Arranging
These flowers are in such pretty colours they can either be arranged in a small container on their own or a few stems may be added to a mixed vase.

Preparation
Dip stem ends in boiling water then give a long drink.

Nemesia strumosa suttoni

Nemophila

insignis   20 cm

A wonderful blue, this little annual provides a fresh shade of colour for the cool, moist border.
It may be sown direct out of doors in April and will flower from June until the autumn.

Arranging
This flower does not seem to be grown by many arrangers which is such a pity, as it looks absolutely enchanting in miniature arrangements or in little posies. It really earns its nickname of baby blue eyes.

Preparation
A diagonal cut and a long drink.

Nepeta

x *faassenii (mussinii)*   30 cm

The lavender shaded spikes of this perennial make the plant a favourite for border edging, either along rose beds or in front of other herbaceous or annual plants. The first flush of flowers on grey stems, in May and June is the most beautiful, but flowering continues intermittently until September. The plants do best in full sun on well drained soil.
Plants may be raised from seed sown outdoors in May or June to flower the next year and once a stock has been raised, division or basal cuttings in early spring will maintain plant supplies.

Arranging
I do enjoy using these long lasting blue-grey spikes mixed in with pink flowers. I feel they are a must for the arranger and my cats agree with me!

Preparation
No special treatment.

Nepeta x faassenii

Nerine bowdenii

Nerine

bowdenii   50 – 60 cm

This species is perhaps the hardiest of the nerines, but always needs a warm, sheltered border with light, rich soil. The umbels of pink flowers in September and October are so beautiful and so welcome that it is worth taking the necessary extra trouble to grow this bulbous herbaceous plant, which first came to us from South Africa.

Plant bulbs outdoors in spring, in a very well prepared bed, some 15 cm deep. The flower spikes begin to show in September and at this time water the bed if the weather is dry. After flowering, cover the bed with litter of dry bracken. They dislike disturbance, but welcome a spring mulch of well rotted compost.

The bulbs also lend themselves to growing in pots or tubs for patio or cool conservatory. In this case, set the bulbs again in light rich compost, with their tops just showing above soil level. The leaves will appear first, and once these die down, no water should be given until the flower buds start to show in August.

Arranging

This attractive flower, a single head of which can be arranged either just with a stark branch, or with grey foliage, also blends well with the pastel shades of asters and dahlias.

Preparation

A diagonal cut and then a long drink.

Nicotiana

affinis 'Evening Fragrance'   90 cm
affinis 'Lime Green'   80 cm

Like the night-scented stock these tobacco plants have a wonderful scent as the day cools. The first variety comes in a number of shades from white to pink, crimson and purple, the second, true to its name, is a delicate light green.

Start the seed indoors in March. Handle the tiny seedlings carefully and grow on until the plants can be set outside in late May or early June. They do best on good soil and tolerate shade, flowering on branching stems from July until the autumn.

A great advantage in some new strains is their ability to open during daylight hours and still retain their fragrance.

Arranging

How popular this plant has become. The lime green variety looks so refreshing in a green arrangement set in a shallow dish with some stones in the water. The varieties in other shades add beauty to any summer mixed group.

Preparation

A diagonal cut and a warm drink.

Olearia

x *haastii*   AGM   1 m

One of the New Zealand daisy bushes, this neat little evergreen is perhaps the most adaptable species in our country, revelling in dry situations and greeting each summer with a mass of starry, cream coloured flowers.

The leaves are evergreen and very tolerant of sea breezes or industrial pollution.

Little pruning is required as the bush is of close habit and will make a good hedge.

Propagate by half ripened wood cuttings in a cold frame.

Arranging

I like to use the daisy-like flowers to mix in with other white material in mid-summer. The glossy foliage is an added bonus.

Preparation
Peel off lower bark and give a warm drink.

Osmanthus delavayi

Osmanthus

delavayi AGM	1·5 m
heterophyllus (ilicifolius)	1·8 m

Fragrant shrubs from China and Japan, the osmanthus are evergreen, slow growing and densely twiggy. Eminently suitable for a small garden where they provide shelter, background and small fragrant, white blossoms, *O. delavayi* in April and *O. hetero-phyllus* in September and October. They flower while still quite young bushes and thrive on most soils.
Pruning is rarely needed as they are of neat habit.
Half ripened wood cuttings should root in a cold frame.

Arranging
The beautiful glossy foliage is perfect as a background for other blossoms. It is also nice to use when clothed

with its own fragrant tubular flowers.

Preparation
Hammer or split stem ends and give a long drink.

Pachysandra

terminalis AGM	20 – 30 cm
terminalis 'Variegata'	20 cm

This is a humble, good natured ground cover plant from Japan, asking little but some sort of soil in which to grow, often enough in semi-shade under the shrubs or to cover areas round newly erected office blocks in industrial sites. Small, whitish flowers open on the shoots in spring.
No pruning is needed and plants may be divided in autumn. When first planting out, give 10 cm space apart.

Arranging
This is one of the longest lasting materials in water. Being evergreen it provides a constant source of foliage which is especially welcome for use with the early small spring bulbs.

Preparation
A diagonal cut and a good drink. Leaves can be pressed.

Pachysandra terminalis

Paeonia lactiflora

Paeonia

lactiflora hybrids		1·2 m
mlokosewitschii	AGM	60 cm
officinalis		1 m
delavayi hybrids		1·6 m
lutea ludlowii	AGM	2 m
suffruticosa hybrids		1·5 m

Peonies are divided into two groups, the first and better known are all herbaceous, dying down to ground level in winter. Give them the best possible soil, deeply cultivated and well manured. Choose a spot from which they need not be moved, for they dislike disturbance. They will grow equally well on limy soil if preparation has been thorough. Mulch round the plants in winter.

Plant in autumn or early spring a metre apart, with crown buds no more than 5 cm below the surface. *P. lactiflora* and *P. officinalis* are parent species for most fine pink, white and crimson varieties flowering in May and June. *P. mlokosewitschii* was discovered in the Caucasus mountains. It flowers in April with bright, lemon-yellow single flowers.

The second group includes the tree peonies which thrive in sunny sheltered sites on limy or other well drained soil. Their handsome deciduous leaves are attractive all the summer and flowers, often single, open in May.

Little pruning is required.

Mixed hybrids may be raised from seed sown in spring. Tree peonies are often grafted.

Arranging

These flowers provide good substantial material which enhances any large summer vase. They are particularly useful for church and marquee groups.

Preparation

When I have gathered the flowers I put them in a polythene bag on a cold floor and leave them overnight. Then I cut the stem ends diagonally and give them a long warm drink.

Papaver orientalis 'Goliath'

Papaver

nudicaule (Iceland poppy)	50 cm
orientalis	75 cm
rhoeas	60 cm
somniferum	60 cm

In one form or another, poppies are well known to us all. The four species chosen here include:

P. rhoeas, the red annual from which hybrids in

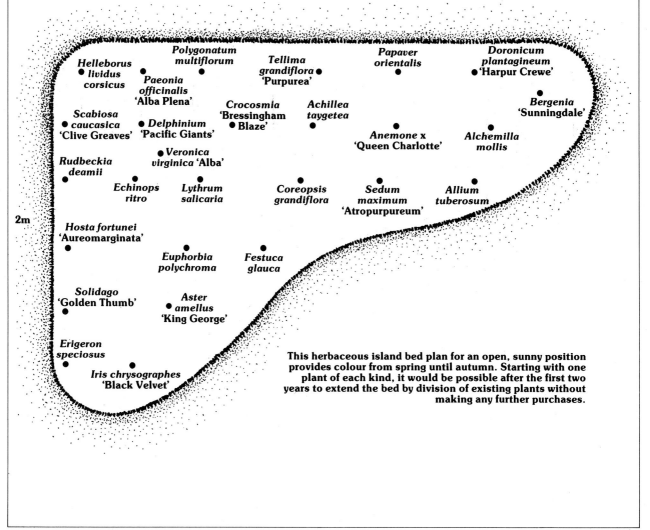

3m

2m

Helleborus lividus corsicus

Polygonatum multiflorum

Tellima grandiflora 'Purpurea'

Papaver orientalis

Doronicum plantagineum 'Harpur Crewe'

Paeonia officinalis 'Alba Plena'

Scabiosa caucasica 'Clive Greaves'

Delphinium 'Pacific Giants'

Crocosmia 'Bressingham Blaze'

Achillea taygetea

Bergenia 'Sunningdale'

Anemone x 'Queen Charlotte'

Alchemilla mollis

Rudbeckia deamii

Veronica virginica 'Alba'

Echinops ritro

Lythrum salicaria

Coreopsis grandiflora

Sedum maximum 'Atropurpureum'

Allium tuberosum

Hosta fortunei 'Aureomarginata'

Euphorbia polychroma

Festuca glauca

Solidago 'Golden Thumb'

Aster amellus 'King George'

Erigeron speciosus

Iris chrysographes 'Black Velvet'

This herbaceous island bed plan for an open, sunny position provides colour from spring until autumn. Starting with one plant of each kind, it would be possible after the first two years to extend the bed by division of existing plants without making any further purchases.

beautiful pastel shades have been raised. Seed of this species is sown in spring, on any light soil, to flower throughout the summer.

P. nudicaule, with leafless stems, is best treated as a biennial, the seed being sown in June to flower the next summer. The shades are from creamy white to yellow, apricot and deep orange.

P. somniferum is annual and sown direct. Its greyish foliage is an attraction as well as the single and double pink shaded flowers.

P. orientalis was originally a huge, gay red perennial but many selected named varieties in other shades are now available. Plants grow happily on any good border soil and flower from June to August. Stems need staking to prevent flopping.

Named varieties are increased from root cuttings in early spring.

Arranging

Because of their short life once picked, I only use these gorgeous splashes of colour in special big arrangements when I really want to make an impact.

Preparation

You must either burn or scald the stem ends before giving a long cold drink, and gather just as they are opening. Dry green seed heads by standing them upright in a vase.

Passiflora

caerulea   4 m

So unusually beautiful are these passion flowers it is

worth making an effort to try to grow a plant on a south facing wall.

Seed may be sown indoors in spring and a plant set out when a year old. Given warm conditions and well drained soil, it will often make rampant growth, climbing over and through other bushes and delighting quite suddenly with its first open flower. In hot summers, the climbing stems are gay with orange, edible fruits in autumn.

Prune quite hard in spring, removing the long trails almost to their bases and trim if necessary during the summer too.

Arranging

I can remember as a child being shown a wall of these absolutely beautiful flowers and vowing to myself that I would one day have my own wall covered with passiflora. That day has come. What a joy the stems and blossoms are to arrange in a fruit and flower group.

Preparation

Trail ends should be dipped in boiling water and then the whole of the material should be submerged in cold water for a few hours.

Pernettya

mucronata   AGM   1 m
mucronata 'Alba'   1 m

These attractive little evergreen shrubs associate well with heathers and dwarf rhododendrons, needing the same lime free soil and lots of peat and leaf-mould. They are hardy, coming from the extreme south of South America. Their tiny leaves are shiny, the white flowers in spring like lily of the valley and the pink or white round berries are a delight throughout the winter. They will succeed in partial shade, but fruit best in sunny sites. Plant male and female bushes to ensure pollination for berry production.

No pruning is needed.

New plants may be raised from stratified seed or from natural suckers.

Arranging

The berried sprays in autumn make rather a nice subject to mix in with some of the autumnal flowers such as spray chrysanthemums, dahlias and michaelmas daisies.

Preparation

Hammer stem ends and give a good drink.

Perovskia

atriplicifolia 'Blue Spire'   AGM   1 m

This little shrub should be much more widely planted for it succeeds in any well drained soil on a sunny site. The foliage and stems are grey. Soft blue flowers open in August and September.

It would be lovely planted on a sunny patio or on grey or blue borders.

Prune the flowered shoots back in spring, to low buds.

Take cuttings of young wood in summer to root in a cold frame. Soft stemmed cuttings may also be rooted indoors in spring.

Arranging

These violet-blue spiky stems will add to the outline of a late summer mixed vase. They are particularly pretty arranged with pink flowers.

Preparation

Hammer or split stem ends and give a good drink.

Perovskia atriplicifolia

The well-loved mock orange

Philadelphus

'Beauclerk'	AGM	1·6 m
'Belle Etoile'	AGM	1·6 m
'Burfordensis'		2·1 m
coronarius 'Aureus'		1·1 m
'Sybille'	AGM	1·4 m
'Virginal'	AGM	3 m

This genus of mock orange shrubs should find a home in every garden. The beautiful white flowers are fragrant and charming in June and July.

Easy to grow, even on limy or dry soils, this shrub becomes unsightly and straggly unless controlled by pruning out the flowered stems to low buds as soon as blossoms fade. (Not an easy task to fit in when so much else has to be done in July and August). Where a bush has grown too tall, it is best to cut low into old wood and lose a year's blossom.

Propagation is easy by hard wood cuttings in autumn.

P. 'Belle Etoile' and *P.* 'Sybille' have fringed petals, and *P. coronarius* 'Aureus' has golden foliage in spring. *P.* 'Virginal' is pure white and double.

Arranging

This shrub is one of my special favourites, the flowers are so dainty and look perfect in a wedding group. Smaller pieces mix in well with all delicate looking summer flowers.

Preparation

Remove as many surplus leaves as possible, then hammer stem ends and give a warm drink. It helps to scrape off the lower 6 cm of bark.

Phlox

drummondii	30 cm
paniculata (decussata)	90 cm

The annual *P. drummondii* in many gay shades of pink, white, salmon and red, is sown indoors in March for planting outside in sunny borders in May. The flowering season extends to late September.

Perennial varieties of *P. paniculata* need good deep soil, for they are hungry plants. They also need ample moisture so a damp part of the border is best. They are mainly summer and autumn flowering with a wide range of strong shades.

Propagation is best by root cuttings.

When replanting, always choose a completely fresh site to avoid infection from eelworm and never take cuttings from any but healthy looking plants.

Arranging

As arrangers we are so lucky to have the variation in size provided by this genus. The tall stems of *P. paniculata,* with their rounded heads of flowers, are

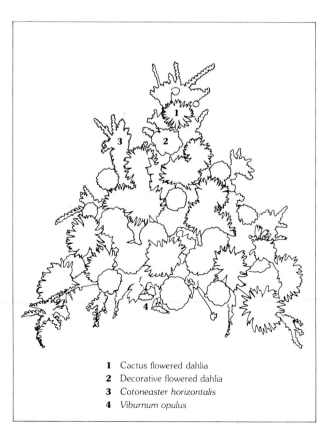

1	Cactus flowered dahlia
2	Decorative flowered dahlia
3	*Cotoneaster horizontalis*
4	*Viburnum opulus*

very valuable and long lasting in large mixed summer vases. The shorter stems of *P. drummondii* look effective in smaller containers.

Preparation
Hammer stem ends and give a warm drink.

A variety of *Phlox paniculata*

Phormium

'Bronze Baby'	60 cm
cookianum	60 cm – 1·5 m
tenax 'Purpureum'	2 m
tenax 'Variegatum'	2 m
tenax 'Veitchii'	1·5 m

The smaller selections of these rather exotic looking New Zealand plants may be grown in large pots or tubs for the patio, when their size will not be as great as indicated above. For open spaces, the varieties of *P. tenax* may grow taller than shown.

The leaves are tough and seem able to withstand much bad weather. Variegated and coloured forms are specially attractive. In really hot seasons the flower spikes of *P. tenax* are eye catching and strangely aromatic.

The tough rootstock may be divided in April. It is probably easier to raise new plants from seed!

Arranging
Nurseries are really pandering to the flower arrangers' love of these beautiful sword shaped leaves. You can always find a use for them throughout the year either as a stark background for a line arrangement or to give a defined shape to a larger group.

Preparation
No special treatment, but I shave the ends to a point before putting them in an arrangement.

Phormium tenax 'Sundowner'

Physalis

alkekengii	30 – 50 cm
franchetii	50 – 60 cm

These Chinese lantern or Cape gooseberry plants are easy to grow in sunny, rich borders and provide useful stems of lantern-like fruits in autumn.

The roots may be divided in spring and once every

three or four years, the site of the bed should be changed to maintain quality growth. Seed saved from the fruits inside the lanterns may also be sown outdoors in spring.

Plants are herbaceous, dying down to the ground in winter, but are better in a bed of their own than in a mixed border.

Arranging

These plants are mostly used in dried form when their lovely orange seed heads add colour to a mixed dry winter group. They are often arranged with honesty, a good idea because you have a complete contrast of shape and colour. Physalis can also be used when the seed heads are green and unripe in a mixed green shaded arrangement.

Preparation

When the seed heads have turned orange, remove all leaves and hang stems upside down to dry.

Physalis alkekengii

Phytolacca

americana   1 – 2 m

This useful and unusual herbaceous plant from North America deserves to be more widely grown by flower arrangers. Perhaps the fact that roots and seeds are poisonous has discouraged its wider use.

The summer flowers in tall spikes are followed by heads of purple-black berries in autumn. At the same season the 15 cm leaves turn from dark green to rich purple, making a striking feature in a flower border.

It is easily raised from seed sown outdoors in spring, or by division at the same season.

Arranging

As this plant produces rather long spikes it is marvellous for really large groups either in its flowering form, or later when it produces heavenly clusters of dark purple berries. The fruit spikes can also be mixed with mauve flowers in a line arrangement, but do not use the berries where there are children.

Preparation

Dip flower stem ends in boiling water and then give a long drink. Remove leaves from berried stems and give them a warm drink.

Pieris

'Forest Flame'   1·5 – 2 m
japonica 'Variegata'   AGM   1 m

These are peat loving bushes to associate with ericas and rhododendrons. A little shade and shelter from other shrubs may prevent spring frosts catching the tender new shoots in April.

The plants are evergreen and in good conditions, will flower in spring with racemes of white blossoms similar to lily of the valley. The other special attraction with *P*. 'Forest Flame' is that early shoots are bright red, later turning from pink to cream and green. The variegated form is slow growing, prettily coloured white and green. Its spring shoots are pink tinted.

Pruning only involves cutting away dead flower heads and trimming straggly shoots back in April.

New plants may be increased by seed or by layering.

Arranging

This is an early spring flowering shrub that, once growing well, will provide the arranger with cascading branches of white flowers and red leaves, perfect to group with so many of the spring flowers.

Preparation
Hammer stem ends and give a long drink.

Pieris japonica

Pittosporum

tenuifolium   3 m

Any well drained soil and a sheltered site will suit this shrub, but only in the milder areas. This is one of the hardier species and is much grown near the sea in the south west. In favoured areas it will grow taller than indicated and make a small tree which being evergreen, creates a good wind-break. The foliage is shiny with wavy edges to each leaf and the dark slender stems form an attractive contrast.
No regular pruning is necessary – only trimming to shape in April.
Half ripened wood cuttings will root indoors in summer.

Arranging
I wish this shrub were a little more hardy, as the glossy

94

foliage harmonises so well with many kinds of flowers. I use it in pedestals and even introduce little sprigs of three or four leaves into quite tiny vases.

Preparation
Hammer or split stem ends and give a good drink.

Pittosporum tenuifolium 'Silver Queen

Polemonium

caeruleum   70 cm

Shorter selections of this pretty, herbaceous perennial have been made in recent years. All are easy to grow and make an early contribution to colour in the border, opening in May and June. Both flowers and foliage are attractive. The flower spikes do not need staking.
Stock may be divided in spring or seed may be sown indoors or in a cold frame.

Arranging
With a return to cottage flowers, this plant is again becoming popular. I enjoy using the stems, as they give height to smaller arrangements without introducing excessive flower or leaf growth.

Preparation
A diagonal cut and a good drink.

Polemonium caeruleum

Polygonatum multiflorum

Polygonatum

multiflorum   AGM   60 cm

The Solomon's seal plant is associated with cottage gardens and the stems have a graceful arching habit all their own. The well spaced bells hang from these stems.

Cool soil in sunny or shady sites will suit this hardy herbaceous perennial which flowers in May and June.

The long tuberous roots form colonies after a while. The plants can be divided in autumn or early spring.

Arranging

What a graceful line this plant produces, making it a perfect addition to any group which requires some arching sprays.

Preparation

A diagonal cut and a long drink. This material benefits from being sprayed with a water mister. Preserve leaves by the glycerine method for a few days then hang them upside down to dry.

Polygonum

affine 'Donald Lowndes' AGM	25 cm
amplexicaule 'Atrosanguineum'	1·2 m
bistorta 'Superbum' AGM	90 cm
baldschuanicum AGM	6 m

The first three named are selections from the herbaceous perennial species in this genus. They grow easily and are suited to different areas of the garden. The shortest is ideal for a sunny patch on rock garden or patio. Its small pink flower spikes keep coming all the summer.

The tallest makes almost a bush among herbaceous plants and flowers with small crimson spikes well into the autumn.

P. bistorta 'Superbum' is best in moist areas, near a water garden. Its large leaves, not unlike dock, set off the deep pink spikes of flowers from July to September.

All these species divide readily in spring.

The fourth species is a quite rampant climber, invaluable for screening a fence or shed or unsightly structure, and growing metres a year. It also bears a generous covering of creamy flower panicles during summer, adding charm to the shiny foliage and twisting stems. It may grow much higher than 6 m if allowed to twine through a tall tree. Full sunshine is more important than soil type. Usually fairly hardy, coming from the colder areas of Bokhara in Turkey, it is sometimes cut to the ground in winter.

As a precaution it is wise to root a few half ripened wood cuttings in a cold frame in summer to serve as replacements. Prune hard back in spring if too rampant.

It is strange to think all these polygonums are cousins to our ubiquitous weeds – persicaria and knot grass.

Arranging
The climbing species is a valuable plant for the arranger who can gather *P. baldschuanicum* like mad and still it keeps making new flowers. The whole heads can be used in larger groups or they can be broken down for small vases, either way they do last very well. The other varieties provide spiky shapes which can be added to mixed vases.

Preparation
Dip stem ends into boiling water then give a long drink.

Potentilla fruticosa can be used as an attractive hedge

Potentilla

fragiformis	15 cm
fruticosa	1 m

In this genus are several herbaceous and many shrubby species. All are hardy, easy to grow, useful plants for the garden. They succeed in sun or shade but flower best in full sunshine.

P. fragiformis is herbaceous with silky leaves and in spring, large flowers.

P. fruticosa is shrubby and makes a dense bush with small, divided leaves and a host of golden blossoms from May until the autumn. It will make a pretty hedge and we have successfully grown it in this way interplanted with *Spiraea* x *b.* 'Anthony Waterer', alongside a gravel drive. We have cut it all to ground level in February or March and thus maintained a regular supply of young flowering stems about 60 cm tall.

Prune out old wood in early spring. Plants may be

Polygonum baldschuanicum

grown from seed or from division.

Varieties of *P. fruticosa* may be apricot, cream or orange shades.

Arranging

These bright little flowers, produced so freely on branches clothed in leafy green, make a charming addition to any summer or autumn vase. The yellow varieties particularly, provide a splash of sunlight in an arrangement.

Preparation

Dip stem ends into boiling water for a few minutes then give a long drink.

Poterium obtusum

Poterium

obtusum	75 cm
sitchense (Sanguisorba rubra)	1 m

Ordinary soil, sunny or shady borders will suit these burnet plants provided they have ample moisture in summer. They may grow beside water or in damp meadow or woodland.

Both species flower in summer from June to August with pink or red flower spikes which resemble small bottle brushes.

Species may be raised from seed or the plants will divide readily in spring.

Arranging

If you want to break up the line of a flat group, do try using these bottle brushes as their upright or curved shapes are invaluable for this purpose.

Preparation

Dip stem ends in boiling water and then give a long drink.

Primula

auricula	15 cm
denticulata AGM	30 cm
vulgaris (primrose) AGM	12 cm
aurantiaca hybrids	30 cm
bulleyana AGM	60 cm
florindae AGM	70 cm
helodoxa AGM	60 cm
japonica AGM	60 cm
pulverulenta AGM	60 cm
rosea AGM	10 – 15 cm
vialii (littoniana)	50 cm

In special areas of the garden, primula species can provide colour from early spring until the autumn.

The first three species listed will grow in sunny or shady borders but dislike strong summer sunlight. The primrose, *P. vulgaris,* and the mop-headed *P. denticulata* will naturalise in filtered shade.

The other species, coming mainly from the mountain valley areas of eastern Asia, need really damp, peaty conditions to produce their wonderful flowers. *P. rosea* opens in March, closely followed by the magnificent species in the Candelabra section of the genus. These include *P. aurantiaca, P. bulleyana, P. helodoxa, P. japonica,* and *P. pulverulenta.* Their flowers open in tiers, up the stem, over a long period. *P. florindae* and *P. vialii (littoniana)* have terminal heads of blossom and flower in June and July.

Species may be raised from seed, preferably sown as soon as it is ripe. Primroses divide best after flowering.

Arranging

What an attractive genus this is, almost too numerous to mention individually, but all delightful arranged on their own in small containers with their natural leaves.

Primulas enjoy lightly shaded conditions and soil that does not at any time dry out

They can also be mixed in with many other flowers in their season.

Preparation
Dip stem ends into boiling water and then give a long drink.

Prunus

laurocerasus 'Otto Luyken'		1·3 m
lusitanica 'Variegata'		2 m
cerasifera 'Pissardii'	AGM	3 m
davidiana 'Alba'	AGM	3 m
persica		2 m
subhirtella 'Autumnalis'	AGM	4 m
subhirtella 'Autumnalis Rosea'	AGM	4 m
triloba 'Flore Pleno'	AGM	4 m
'Kanzan'	AGM	4 m
'Pink Perfection'		2 – 3 m
'Tai Haku'	AGM	large tree

Prunus is a complex genus including apricot, peach, plum and cherry among the deciduous species and laurel among the evergreens.

Most flower in spring, *P. davidiana* 'Alba' as early as February, and are in pink and white shades. *P. c.* 'Pissardii' has coppery purple leaves throughout the summer and the three Japanese varieties listed – 'Kanzan', 'Pink Perfection' and 'Tai Haku' – are coppery in spring when the shoots open with the blossoms. *P. triloba* 'Flore Pleno' is best seen when trained against a wall with the old flowered shoots pruned out straight after flowering.

The two evergreens, *P. l.* 'Otto Luyken', a small laurel, and *P. lusitanica* 'Variegata', a form of Portuguese laurel, make useful wind-breaks and background colour throughout the year.

Of the varieties listed, *P.* 'Kanzan' and *P.* 'Tai Haku' are suitable only for larger gardens.

P. persica, the peach, is always subject to leaf curl disease and should be sprayed in February to ward off attacks.

P. subhirtella 'Autumnalis' really gives delight when

its delicate flowers begin to open in October and are to be found off and on during any mild winter spells. All the prunus species enjoy well drained neutral or limy soil. In the main they are best left unpruned with the exception of fruiting and wall trained species.

The majority are budded onto a rootstock but the evergreens and *P. c.* 'Pissardii' can be raised from hard wood cuttings in autumn.

Arranging

When I do a large arrangement in which I have included sprays of flowering cherry, I really feel spring has arrived. Alternatively you can just use small pieces mixed with other spring flowers in little vases. The autumn flowering varieties provide the arranger with dainty coloured sprays for special groups. The evergreen varieties give us extremely useful foliage at all seasons.

Preparation

Hammer stem ends or dip in boiling water, then give a long drink.

Prunus lusitanica 'Variegata'

Prunus triloba 'Flore Pleno'

Pyracantha

angustifolia
atalantoides (gibbsii)   AGM
atalantoides 'Aurea' ('Flava')
coccinea 'Lalandei'   AGM
rogersiana 'Flava'   AGM

It is no wonder that these evergreen shrubs, coming originally mainly from China, are so popular. Their berries, so freely produced each year and their adaptability to grow in any soil on almost any site, even in the large cities and alongside busy trunk roads, have endeared them to gardeners everywhere.

Clusters of creamy flowers open in May or June, almost smothering the shiny green leaves for a time. Berries colour in early autumn and last as long as the birds will leave them alone. The bushes are spiny and can make a good informal hedge up to 1·5 – 2 m in height. Trained against a north-east wall, the shrub will reach 3 – 4 m and should then have long shoots trimmed back after flowering. If drastic pruning is necessary, cut hard into old wood in April.

Propagation from stratified seeds in autumn is easy.

The genus dislikes root disturbance and plants are best bought initially in containers.

Arranging

For large church or house groups, what more could

we ask for than these splendid straight or curved branches that provide flowers and berries in season.

Preparation
Spray the berries with clear varnish. Hammer or split stem ends and give a warm drink.

A well-grown specimen plant of pyracantha

Pyrus salicifolia 'Pendula'

Pyrus

salicifolia 'Pendula'   AGM   4 m

Worthy of a place as a specimen tree in any medium sized garden, the willow-leafed pear is beautiful from spring, when its silvery leaves and creamy white flowers open, until autumn when the leaves fall.
It is a grafted tree with weeping habit and seldom needs pruning.

Arranging
A useful grey-leafed tree which provides the arranger with substantial pieces of grey foliage for summer groups.

Preparation
Hammer or split stem ends and give a good drink in warm water.

1 *Chamaecyparis lawsoniana* 'Stewartii'
2 *Taxus baccata*
3 *Juniperus squamata* 'Meyeri'
4 Pyracantha

100

Reseda

odorata   30 cm

Among the fragrant annual flowers, mignonette is as important as night-scented stock and nicotiana. It should always find a place, for the scent is refreshing at all hours of the day.

Sow the seed outdoors on the annual border or just under a window, in April. It will flower with greenish orange spikes of flowers from late June onward.

Arranging
This is another of my childhood favourites as it was one of the first flowers I ever grew myself. I use it in small vases in the summer particularly for its scent and I like to add it to special arrangements in guest bedrooms.

Preparation
A diagonal cut, remove lower leaves and give a good drink. Seed heads should be gathered and hung upside down to dry.

Rhododendron williamsianum

Rhododendron and azalea

Evergreen species and hybrids

R. 'Elizabeth'	AGM	1 – 1·2 m
R. ponticum		2 – 3 m
R. 'Praecox'	AGM	1 – 1·2 m
R. williamsianum		1 m
R. 'Yellow Hammer'		1 – 1·2 m
A. 'Atalanta'		60 cm – 1 m
A. 'Palestrina'	AGM	60 cm – 1 m

Semi-evergreen and deciduous species and hybrids

R. kaempferi	AGM	1 – 2 m
R. luteum (A. pontica)	AGM	1 – 2 m
A. mollis		1 m

Perhaps this extensive genus has a wider colour range and longer flowering period than any other group of shrubs. The gayest season extends from April until June when opening shoots and delicate shades of every hue bring fresh delight. Many are fragrant and in autumn, leaves of many deciduous species develop wonderful fiery colours.

All need lime free, moist, peaty soil. Filtered shade from other shrubs will help to prevent frost damage on young spring growth and provide a wind shield. Annual mulches of bracken or leaf-mould help to retain moisture and maintain acid conditions. In areas of low rainfall, free growth is not always realised although the plants may be persuaded to flower.

No pruning, other than the removal of dead flower heads, is needed. Soft cuttings taken just after the shrubs have flowered, may be rooted in heat.

Arranging
Depending on the rhododendron material available, you can either float individual flower heads or use branches in large arrangements. Smaller pieces can be used , when it is best to remove some of the leaves to reveal the beauty of the flower head. They are also lovely arranged alone.

My favourite way with the deciduous azaleas (now mainly classed with rhododendron) is to choose the apricot and salmon shades to arrange with their own foliage in a copper container.

Preparation
Hammer or split stem ends and give them a really long drink.

Rodgersia

aesculifolia	AGM	1 m
pinnata 'Superba'	AGM	80 cm
podophylla		90 cm
tabularis		1 m

Beautiful plants in foliage and flower for the moist, peaty part of the garden, these plants were introduced from China and Japan about a century ago. The leaves are unusually large, those of *R. aesculifolia* having almost an identical shape to those of a horse chestnut tree. Even the seed pods of *R. p.* 'Superba' are handsome.

Give shelter from strong wind. Divide plants in early spring.

Arranging

These plants provide interesting foliage and charming flowers which can be used either together or separately. When the leaves take on their autumn colouring they are wonderful arranged with a few flowers of similar hues.

Preparation

Dip leaf stem ends into boiling water for a few minutes and then submerge overnight in cold water.

Rodgersia pinnata

many years.

R. banksiae (double yellow) flowers best trained on a warm south facing wall; never quite hardy, it does not flower until the wood is three years old and must have sunshine to ripen up the buds. It is almost thornless and in mild winters, almost evergreen. When newly planted, refrain from pruning at all for three years, until it has settled in.

R. 'Cecile Brunner' is a tiny, perfectly formed double pink rose which can now also be obtained in climbing form. It is almost perpetual flowering during summer and autumn.

R. rubrifolia has pale pink single flowers, and fine hips in autumn but its main attraction is the glaucous red-grey shade of stems and leaves. For this reason it should be given ample space to grow. An added joy is that stems are almost thornless.

R. 'Zephirine Drouhin' has been known as the thornless rose for over a century. In addition it is a warm pink and sweetly scented.

Good soil is needed for all roses and a dressing of bonemeal in early spring. Avoid deep cultivation near the roots. Prune out old unproductive wood as growth begins in spring.

R. rubrifolia may be grown from stratified fruits. The other three may be grown from cuttings but are

Rosa 'Zephirine Drouhin'

Rosa

banksiae	5 m
'Cecile Brunner'	90 cm
rubrifolia AGM	2 m
'Zephirine Drouhin'	2 – 3 m

These are four fine roses which have been with us for

usually budded onto a rootstock.

Arranging
Roses in all their forms are firm favourites with me. If you have one perfect bloom do not be afraid to cut it, place in a specimen vase, and enjoy its beauty – I do! Roses look very good arranged on their own or in mixed vases.

The varieties listed are good to handle, being almost thornless. Little *R.* 'Cecile Brunner' is ideal in miniature arrangements, while the foliage of the species *R. rubrifolia* is always in demand for summer red or pink shaded groups.

Preparation
Split stem ends, give a diagonal cut and a long drink.

If caught by frost, young plants pruned in April will usually break from the base. Older plants are more difficult and it is wise to keep a few heeled cuttings rooting in a cold frame for replacements when these are needed.

Arranging
I like to see a few sprigs of rosemary added to a vase of pastel coloured flowers or to a mixed blue and mauve group.

Preparation
Hammer or split stem ends and give a good drink.

Rosmarinus officinalis

Rudbeckia 'Marmalade'

Rosmarinus

officinalis	1 m

A rather short lived but lovely herb and shrub, grown not only for its grey-blue blossoms which the bees love to visit, but for the evergreen, aromatic foliage. Ideally it grows most happily on sunny, well drained slopes, in light, often chalky soil, preferring a rather warmer climate than England provides. It often grows well in our seaside gardens.

Rudbeckia

'Rustic Dwarfs'	60 cm
'Marmalade'	45 cm
deamii	75 cm
newmanii	60 cm

Here are two annual varieties, the first in shades of yellow and bronze, the second a brilliant orange to bring sunshine into any garden from August to

October. Seed may be sown, indoors in February for planting out in May, or direct on a sunny patch of soil, in April.

Both *R. deamii* and *R. newmanii,* golden daisies with black-eyed centres, are useful in the border giving a different pattern of flower in August and September. They have strong stems and are long lasting on the plants. Try to avoid them being overcrowded by more rampant perennials.

Increase both by division in early spring.

Arranging

These provide a ray of sunshine which will brighten up any mixed summer or autumn vase. Try not to associate them with other daisy shaped flowers.

Preparation

Dip stem ends into boiling water and give a long drink.

Ruta graveolens 'Jackman's Blue' (centre right)

Ruta

graveolens 'Jackman's Blue'	50 cm
graveolens 'Variegata'	45 cm

Rue has a very special colour and foliage shape. Nothing quite matches the calm blue of a rue bush. Sunny sites at the base of shrubs which colour in autumn, or beside pink flowered plants are good for the first all blue variety. The variegated form is almost

a decoration in itself, adding light to the border, although I do not think it has the character of 'Jackman's Blue'. Prune back these little shrubs in April.

Seed may be sown of the former, and cuttings of either will root indoors.

Rue has a bitter taste and some people find themselves allergic to handling both leaves and stems.

Arranging

Because it is evergreen, this is a most useful plant with such beautiful blue leaves. I love to cut sprigs for inclusion in winter groups and I think it is rather nice to arrange with the little spring bulbous flowers.

Preparation

A diagonal cut and a long drink.

Salvia

argentea		60 cm
haematodes	AGM	90 cm
pratensis		60 cm
x superba (virgata nemerosa)	AGM	90 cm
officinalis		90 cm
officinalis 'Icterina'		50 cm
officinalis 'Purpurascens'	AGM	70 cm
officinalis 'Tricolor'		70 cm
splendens		30 cm
horminum		40 cm

This invaluable genus contains annual, herbaceous and sub-shrubby species.

All will grow in any good garden soil, preferably in sunny, well drained sites.

Perhaps the best known flowering salvia is *S. splendens,* the red flowered annual used in bedding schemes. Raised indoors from a February sowing, it is set in the border in May.

S. horminum, also annual with pink, purple and white bracts, may be sown direct outdoors.

Of the herbaceous species, *S. superba,* with its rich purple, long lasting spikes of flower is well named and makes an outstanding contribution to the border. It divides easily in early spring.

S. argentea, grown mainly for the large, hoary grey leaves, and *S. haematodes* with branching flower stems and lovely light blue flowers, are both short-lived perennials but easily raised from seed.

The sub-shrubby *S. officinalis* or garden sage, has several variations with attractively coloured foliage. Each will enhance shrub borders and prove of culinary use. Cuttings may be rooted in a cold frame in summer. The rather straggly bushes may be pruned to shape in April.

Arranging

A very large range of colours is to be found in this genus. Consequently you should always be able to find the right shade to add to any mixed summer vase. The coloured leaf varieties of sage make useful additions to herbal or green shaded arrangements.

Preparation

Dip stem ends in boiling water and give a good drink.

An attractively coloured form of *S. officinalis* associated with ballota and juniper

Sambucus

nigra 'Aurea'	2 m
nigra 'Laciniata'	2 m
racemosa 'Plumosa Aurea'	1·2 m

Good shrubs on any soil, even on chalk, these golden and cut-leafed elder bushes are of great value for their hardiness, their free flowering habit and their coloured, edible crop of berries each autumn.
S. nigra varieties have the well known creamy white flat heads of fragrant flowers in June and blue-black berries in August and September.

The *S. racemosa* variety has conical heads of flowers followed by bright red fruits.

To keep the shrubs neat in a garden, prune each year in March, rather like *Buddleia davidii,* reducing each of the last year's flower stems to the lowest two or three buds.

Propagation is by hard wood cuttings in autumn out of doors. Birds also sow the seeds very freely.

Arranging

The flowers of this shrub, which do tend to have a rather pungent smell, can be used in large groups. However, I prefer to wait until the berries come and then incorporate them into fruit and flower arrangements.

Preparation

Dip stem ends in boiling water and give a good drink.

Lavender cotton used here as a foliage and colour contrast to the neat box hedge

Santolina

chamaecyparissus (incana)		50 cm
chamaecyparissus corsica ('Nana')	AGM	30 cm
virens (viridis)		50 cm

These sub-shrubby little lavender cotton plants from southern Europe grow happily on the sunny edge of a shrub border. They produce a wealth of well covered stems of feathery foliage, making neat mounds to break the hard line of a path or drive. Later in the season small yellow flowers appear, but all species are grown chiefly for their grey (*S. chamaecyparissus*) or green (*S. virens*) foliage.

To keep the bushes neat, prune back these stems to their lowest buds, each April.

Propagation from hard wood cuttings in autumn outdoors is easy.

Arranging
This is a useful winter shrubby plant which provides very dainty grey or green material when foliage is scarce. Use also with small spring flowers.

Preparation
Hammer stem ends and give a long drink. The yellow flowers can be dried by hanging.

Saxifraga fortunei rubrifolia

Saxifraga

fortunei rubrifolia	30 cm
x *urbium* AGM	30 cm
x *urbium* 'Aurea Punctata'	30 cm
primuloides 'Elliott's Variety'	30 cm

These four dainty species are happy on rock garden, patio or border. Even a little shade if the area is not too dry, will suit the well loved *S.* x *urbium*, better known as London pride and its variegated variety *S.*

u. 'Aurea Punctata'. This species flowers with dainty red stemmed heads in May and June.

S. fortunei rubrifolia, also with graceful crimson stems, flowers in September.

All the species can be increased by division.

Arranging
The very smallest encrusted saxifrages are beautiful in tiny alpine flower arrangements. But here we have included a selection of the later, taller species useful for adding to vases with other dainty spring or early summer flowers.

Preparation
A diagonal cut and a good drink.

Scabiosa

caucasica 'Clive Greaves'	80 cm
atropurpurea nana	50 cm

One of my favourite flowers for many years has been the perennial *S. c.* 'Clive Greaves'. I have cut many hundred slender stems for market and never tired of the beauty of their mauve flowers. They are, however, not put to best use in a border but should be grown in a row in the reserve garden, as here, the plants produce sufficient flowers to cut for effect at least once a week from mid July until October.

Deep fen or other fertile well drained soil, on the alkaline side, is ideal for these plants. The roots are left down for two to three years and should then be divided and planted on a fresh site. The rootstocks become somewhat woody and our best young plants were raised from small green shoots 9 – 12 cm long cut with a sliver of old root in April and planted for one year in nursery rows before final planting out 40 cm apart.

The annual scabious, dwarf mixed double, come in many shades of cream, pink and crimson and if sown in early spring will flower in late summer. The seeds may also be sown in June when the little plants are treated as biennials to be planted out in autumn for flowering the following summer.

Arranging
What appealing flowers these are. I thoroughly enjoy using them in mixed summer vases in pastel shades. They look equally beautiful on their own in a silver container with just a little additional foliage.

Preparation
A diagonal cut and a long drink in warm water.

Schizostylis coccinea 'Major'

Schizostylis

coccinea   60 cm

This slender autumn flowering plant from South Africa is best grown on a warm, sunny and sheltered border. It does not need lifting in winter but welcomes a cover of light bracken litter during the coldest months.

The rhizomes are first planted in early spring. Flowers open in October, several on each slim stem, not unlike small gladioli, but each flower is rather more starry.

The plants may also be grown in pots in a cool greenhouse or conservatory. Set them in winter, protect in a cold frame until spring, then plunge the pots outdoors for the roots to grow on naturally, until September. Bring the pots into the conservatory for the flowering period. Re-pot into fresh soil for the next year.

S. coccinea has a pretty pink form 'Mrs. Hegarty' which may be grown as outlined above. The roots may be divided in spring or new plants can be grown slowly to flowering size from seed.

Arranging
These star-shaped flowers which last well in water, make a nice change from the rather flat headed blooms of autumn. Use them in mixed vases to give contrasting shapes.

Preparation
A diagonal cut and good drink.

Scilla

sibirica   20 cm

This rich blue scilla is one of the most popular early spring flowering bulbs. We have a colony planted under a *Forsythia* 'Lynwood' as they bloom together to make a most attractive combination. They are also happy in grass among our naturalised crocus and triteleia. This scilla increases slowly and does not need to be disturbed.

Arranging
Either incorporate these little blue flowers into a moss garden or arrange them in a small container with the other dainty bulbous spring blooms.

Preparation
A diagonal cut and a good drink.

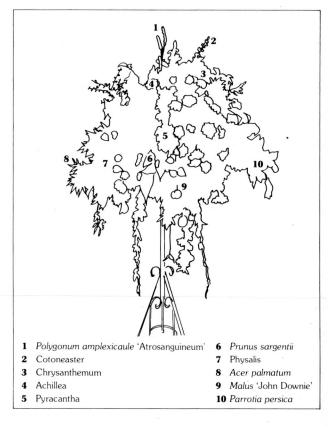

1 *Polygonum amplexicaule* 'Atrosanguineum'	**6**	*Prunus sargentii*
2 Cotoneaster	**7**	Physalis
3 Chrysanthemum	**8**	*Acer palmatum*
4 Achillea	**9**	*Malus* 'John Downie'
5 Pyracantha	**10**	*Parrotia persica*

Sedum spectabile 'Autumn Joy'

Sedum

aizoon 'Aurantiacum'		30 cm
maximum 'Atropurpureum'	AGM	60 cm
rosea (rhodiola)		25 cm
'Ruby Glow'	AGM	25 cm
spectabile 'Autumn Joy'		60 cm
spectabile 'Iceberg'		30 cm
telephium 'Variegatum'		40 cm

Several of the larger sedums are invaluable in the herbaceous border, by virtue of either their coloured leaves or their beautiful flower heads, or both. Stems and leaves of S. *maximum* 'Atropurpureum' are deep purple while the cool glaucous green foliage of S. *spectabile* varieties lends another dimension to a mixed planting. The autumn flower heads rival buddleias and michaelmas daisies in attracting many coloured butterflies.

The smaller species fit happily into the rock garden. Sedums are fairly easy to grow, and withstand dry conditions but do not enjoy being overcrowded.

The rootstocks can be divided, or cuttings of young shoots may be taken, in early spring.

Arranging
As stems of plants in this genus last for a long time in water, the larger species make an invaluable addition to autumn arrangements. The rich red flower heads of S. s. 'Autumn Joy' with sprays of September berries, or the deep red stems and leaves of S. *maximum* 'Atropurpureum', with pink asters or dahlias, make striking focal points. S. *rosea* is a

valuable asset in spring when many other kinds of foliage are too young and tender to cut.

Preparation
A diagonal cut of stem ends and a long drink. Ripe seed heads can be dried by hanging them upside down.

Senecio

cineraria 'Ramparts'	80 cm
cineraria 'White Diamond'	50 cm
greyi AGM	1 m
leucostachys	60 cm

All these species are grown for their grey or white foliage. All do best in sunny well drained sites. The New Zealand species S. *greyi* has oval grey leaves and during the summer, starry yellow daisy flowers. Foliage of the shrub remains brighter if flower stems are cut out. It is evergreen except in really cold winters when it may not prove to be fully hardy. Usually pruning in April will keep the bushes shapely and well covered with foliage. Propagation is by hard wood cuttings.

The other three species are not quite so shrubby but have much whiter, downier leaves and stems. Cuttings may be rooted in a cold frame in summer, and over-wintered in the frame.

Arranging
This genus provides invaluable grey foliage which can be used with many different flowers. S. *greyi* has the added bonus of being available all the year round and I use its stems in many mixed groupings.

Preparation
Hammer stem ends of woody varieties and give a long drink. Stem ends of soft stemmed varieties should be dipped in boiling water for ten seconds and then given a long drink.

Sidalcea

malvaeflora varieties	1 m

Sidalcea is a useful herbaceous perennial with flowers in shades of pink and crimson from June to August. All varieties have upright spikes with glossy mallow-like leaves at the base. Keep the dead flower heads cut off to encourage more stems to develop.

Senecio greyi flanked by, amongst others, mahonia and digitalis

The plants need good soil with ample moisture. Named varieties may be divided in spring. Mixed hybrids can be raised from seed sown in a cold frame to flower the following and subsequent years.

Arranging
This is quite a useful softly coloured species which is ideal for mixing with other summer flowers.

Preparation
Dip stem ends into boiling water for a few minutes then give a long drink. Hang seed heads upside down to dry.

Sisyrinchium

angustifolium	25 cm
striatum	60 cm
striatum 'Variegatum'	45 cm

These little American plants are easily grown in border or rock garden. They are perennial and may be divided in spring or grown from seed. The foliage is sword-like but slender. Flowering continues from June until the autumn.
The variety *S. s.* 'Variegatum' has cream variegation on the foliage.

Arranging
As the flower does not last very well in its fresh state, it is better to use the green seed heads in arrangements. Dry them as they turn almost black and then incorporate the stems in a vase with berries and autumnal flowers.

Preparation
Dip flower stem ends into boiling water and then give a long drink. Hang seed heads upside down to dry.

Skimmia

japonica	AGM	1 m
japonica 'Rubella'	AGM	1 m

These little Japanese shrubs have made themselves very much at home here, in shady lime free borders, inland, near the coast and in industrial areas. Their neat, shiny evergreen leaves are always attractive and the flowers are fragrant.
The variety *S. j.* 'Rubella' has rich pink colouring outside the flower buds.
As male and female flowers are on separate plants, both types must be set together to ensure a crop of bright red, persistent berries for autumn and winter.

No pruning is usually needed, the shrubs being of neat habit.

Low branches may be layered, or berries stratified. Soft wood cuttings may also be rooted indoors.

Arranging
Stems of this shrub with their beautiful shiny leaves show off flowers well. Skimmia can also be used with its own bright red berries in winter or its creamy coloured flowers in early summer.

Preparation
Hammer or split stem ends and give a long cold drink.

Skimmia japonica

Solidago

| 'Golden Thumb' AGM | 30 cm |
| 'Mimosa' | 1·5 – 2 m |

Here is a choice between short and tall varieties of golden rod, those useful herbaceous plants which flower at the same time as michaelmas daisies. They will succeed in any mixed border, doing rather better where the soil is in good heart.

Plants are readily increased by division in spring.

Arranging
There are now tall and smaller much more manageable sized varieties available and I do enjoy using both. The flowers last well in water and give a definite outline to large arrangements. They can also be used in mixed vases.

Preparation
Strip off lower leaves, hammer stem ends lightly, then give a good drink.

Solidago 'Golden Thumb'

Sorbus

aria 'Lutescens' AGM	9 m
cashmiriana	6 m
hupehensis AGM	6 m

These are small trees grown for their attractive foliage, creamy white flowers in late spring and autumn fruit. Like the mountain ash and whitebeam, to which they are related, they will grow in any well drained soil either in town or country and never take up too great a breadth of space.

S. hupehensis and *S. cashmiriana* have neat compound leaves which turn brilliant shades in autumn. Both have white or pinkish berries, less attractive to the birds than the orange ones of the mountain ash, and so hanging longer in autumn. *S. aria* 'Lutescens' has simple leaves which open in spring with a covering of yellowish white down. Later in the season the leaves turn green on the upper surface and grey on the under sides.

Plants may be increased by stratified seed although resultant seedlings may not always be identical with the parent. Cuttings and layers may also be rooted. None of these sorbus normally require pruning. They are happy as specimen trees or bushes, or grown among other shrubs.

Arranging
These small trees prove useful to the arranger because they provide flowering branches to add to summer

arrangements and later, berried stems which are so attractive with red shaded autumn flowers.

Preparation
Hammer or split stem ends and give a good drink.

Sorbus aria 'Lutescens'

Spiraea

x *arguta*	AGM		2 m
x *bumalda* 'Anthony Waterer'	AGM		90 cm
x *bumalda* 'Goldflame'			80 cm

Every garden should find a place for at least one of these dainty spiraeas. They will grow on almost any soil, preferring sunny situations.

S. x *arguta* sometimes known as bridal wreath – a name which aptly describes the neat arrangement of clustered tiny flowers on slender, wiry stems – opens in May just in time for the last narcissus. Flowering on the previous year's wood, it may be cut back straight after the flowers are over.

S. x *b.* 'Anthony Waterer' makes a neat low hedge if cut just above ground level in early spring. It flowers in August with flat heads of crimson blossom. We interplant it with yellow flowered potentilla bushes. The third variety also has crimson flowers but is primarily grown for its warm gold spring foliage which later turns yellow.

All three may be increased by hard wood cuttings in autumn.

Arranging
What dainty flowering sprays these shrubs produce. *S.* x *arguta* is an absolute must for a spring wedding group! I also cut down large pieces and add the small sprays to table arrangements. They combine so well with all types of flowers.

Preparation
Hammer stem ends and give a good drink of warm water. Seed heads can be cut, their foliage removed and the stems stood in 3 cm of water and allowed to dry off in a warm dry atmosphere.

Spiraea x *arguta*

Stachys

lanata 'Sheila Macqueen'	30 – 45 cm
lanata 'Silver Carpet' AGM	10 cm
macrantha (Betonica)	50 cm

Hare's ears we sometimes called *S. lanata*, for the leaves are grey felted and feel so smooth. *S. l.* 'Sheila Macqueen' has larger leaves than the species and finer flower spikes in June, July and August. It grows happily on the sunny edge of a border. *S. l.* 'Silver Carpet' is a low growing variety which seldom flowers and will form a carpet for a corner of the patio or alongside a sunny path. *S. macrantha*, the wood betony, is a good border plant, flowering from May to July with purple spikes above deep green, handsome leaves.

All will grow in almost any well drained soil and may be easily divided in spring. After wet weather the grey foliage should be trimmed to remove the draggled leaves.

Arranging

When using *S. lanata* be very careful not to get the part above the water line wet, as the silky grey leaves become green and lose their charm. I use the grey variety as a backcloth for pink or white flowers.

Stachys lanata rather hemmed in by surrounding ground cover

Preparation

Remove lower leaves, hammer or split stem ends and give a good drink. When seed heads have formed gather and hang them upside down to dry.

Sternbergia

| lutea | 15 cm |

A bulb from the Middle East, sternbergia flowers in autumn with most beautiful crocus-like golden yellow flowers and deep green foliage. Give the bulbs a sunny bank or plant in the shelter of a south facing wall about 10 cm deep, in early spring.

They will increase naturally and need not be disturbed for a number of years, until it is obvious that the area is over crowded. A mossy saxifrage may be over planted to protect the bulbs and provide an attractive background.

New plantings may be made from offsets when the bed is replanted on a fresh site. The bulbs may also be grown in pots of light, rich compost in a cold greenhouse or conservatory.

Arranging

The appearance of these bulbous flowers in November makes me imagine just for a moment that spring is coming! I like to cut a few and put them in a small cut glass vase, as I feel they deserve to stand in splendid isolation.

Preparation

A diagonal cut and a good drink.

Stokesia

| laevis 'Blue Star' AGM | 45 cm |

This pretty blue daisy grows on branching flower stems from a neat mound of dark green foliage. It is an attractive addition to the late summer herbaceous border, flowering from July until September.

New plants may be raised from seed, by division or by root cuttings.

Arranging

This is a long lasting flower in a very pretty shade of blue. As it comes at a time when there are few daisy-like flowers in that colour, it makes a good addition to a late summer vase of pastel shades.

Preparation

Very lightly hammer stem ends and give a long drink.

Stranvaesia

davidiana AGM   3 m

This useful, vigorous shrub, introduced from China less than a century ago quickly found a home here, growing in almost any but the heaviest soils and tolerating semi-shade and industrial pollution. It is evergreen, not unlike a large cotoneaster in habit, with heads of white flowers in June, followed by persistent scarlet fruits. Often the older leaves also turn scarlet in autumn.

No pruning is necessary unless a straggly branch appears. Trim such growths back in April.

Seedlings may be raised from stratified seed.

Arranging
This is a valuable flowering and berrying shrub which is evergreen into the bargain. It provides the arranger with reliable material all the year round.

Preparation
Hammer or split stem ends and give a long drink.

Snow berry

Symphoricarpos

orbiculatus 'Variegatus'   1·2 m
rivularis (albus laevigatus) AGM   1·5 m

The snow berry species are deciduous, hardy and adaptable. They will make dense thickets in woodland and *S. rivularis* thrives under quite heavy tree cover.

They also grow in almost any soil.

Their chief attraction is the winter crop of berries, pink in the first species and white in the second. In addition *S. o.* 'Variegatus' has dainty green leaves variegated gold.

Cut out the oldest stems each year and if very crowded, thin the weakest shoots. This can be done any time during winter.

New plants may be grown from suckers, cuttings or stratified berries.

Arranging
These two species provide you with a choice of pink or white berries, either of which looks so effective cascading over the sides and front of a vase. They also provide a clear colour contrast to the normal shades of scarlet berries used in autumn arrangements.

Preparation
Hammer or split stem ends and give a long drink.

Syringa

vulgaris 'Maud Notcutt'   3 m
vulgaris 'Primrose'   1·3 m
x *prestoniae* 'Bellicent'   AGM   3·5 m

Lilac fragrance is well known all over the country. The shrubs are vigorous and will grow in almost any soil, especially over chalk. Flowers open from early May to late June. The three listed here are all single with their flowers borne in graceful heads. All do best in full sun.

Pruning is mainly to cut off seed heads and to remove stems which have flowered. To keep the bushes from becoming too leggy the new growths may be pinched or stopped to cause them to branch. Should a bush become really tall and bare, it may be cut down to 60 – 90 cm in early spring, losing that season's blossom but making a compact bush for the next year.

New plants may be raised by layering. Sometimes half ripened wood cuttings will root in a cold frame.

Arranging
Contrary to popular belief, if you prepare syringa thoroughly it will last quite well. I love to use large pieces mixed with other May flowering shrubs in pedestal arrangements, but I also enjoy using small spikes arranged in a vase on their own.

Preparation
Remove leaves from flowering spikes, hammer stem

ends well and give a long warm drink. To use foliage, prepare sprays of leaves only, by the same method.

Preparation

Strip off lower leaves, give a diagonal cut and a good drink.

Hybrid marigolds, dependable annuals with a prolonged flowering life

Tagetes

| patula 'Dainty Marietta' | 15 cm |
| patula 'Crackerjack' | 60 cm |

These cheerful half hardy annuals may be sown in March indoors, hardened off in cold frames to plant outdoors in May. A sunny site is best and flowers continue to open as long as dead heads are cut off promptly.

An interesting new race of hybrid Afro-French marigolds has been introduced recently giving larger flowers – (5 – 7 cm across) – more like the African varieties on stems only 25 – 35 cm high. As this race is sterile, blooms are produced well into the autumn. Seed sowing is the same as outlined above.

Arranging

These bright, vibrant coloured heads really look best arranged in a brown basket or pottery container on their own. As they are so stiff, make sure your Oasis comes above the container lip so that you can put some stems in at an angle.

Tamarix

| pentandra | 2·5 m |
| tetrandra | 3·5 m |

Lovely pink flowered shrubs to grace our spring and autumn borders, the tamarix are hardy in exposed coastal areas and prefer well drained light soils to heavy clay. They also prefer sunshine to shade.

Prune the autumn flowering species, *T. pentandra,* in early spring,,like *Buddleia davidii,* down to low buds. The spring flowering species may be shortened back after flowering to encourage new growths for the next year's flowers.

Tamarix may be increased from half ripened wood cuttings in a cold frame in summer.

Tamarix pentandra

We have *T. pentandra* forty-five years old within 30 m of an exposed Norfolk cliff top, growing new shoots every summer and in favourable years, flowering in autumn. The bitter north and east winds effectively prune it back each winter. All we need to do is remove the dead twigs once growth begins.

Arranging
These species have such dainty flowers and foliage that they make a perfect foil for some of the more delicate looking flowers of high summer and autumn.

Preparation
Hammer stem ends and give a good drink.

Tanacetum densum amanum (right) backed by helianthemum and *Genista hispanica*

Tanacetum

densum amanum   15 cm
   (Chrysanthemum poterifolium) (densum)

This lovely grey carpeting plant, with small, silvery feather-like leaves needs a dry, sunny border or patio corner. It flowers but little, with yellow daisy-like heads in summer.
Reasonably hardy in dry conditions, the plant looks sad and straggly in wet seasons and needs careful

trimming to encourage new growths.
It may be raised from cuttings in summer or from rooted layers.

Arranging
A very useful small grey foliage which is a valuable asset for the arranger of miniature vases.

Preparation
Hammer stem ends and give a long drink.

Taxus

baccata   AGM   2 – 2.5 m

The yew is one of our three native conifers which, given well drained soil, will grow in sun or shade, on chalky, acid or neutral areas and will make wind-sturdy hedges fairly quickly. Its dark green foliage is a fine background for light coloured flowering shrubs. Trim yew hedges twice during the growing season – shears may be used. An old tree or hedge may be cut hard back with a saw in April when it will break again from the base.
Yew may be grown from stratified seed or, slowly, from heeled, hard wood cuttings, set outdoors in autumn.
The foliage and fruits are poisonous to grazing stock and human beings. Prunings, even when dry, are still poisonous, so burn the trimmings, never dump where animals may find them.

Arranging
An extremely useful backing material for all sized arrangements. The berried sprays can be used with autumnal flowers such as chrysanthemums.

Preparation
Either hammer or split stem ends and give a good drink.

Teucrium

chamaedrys   30 cm

This native wall germander is a cousin to the wild wood sage. It makes a short, almost evergreen bush with small shiny leaves and may be grown as a low edging to a border in sunny places.
It prefers light, well drained soil and is trimmed back if straggly in April. The pretty spikes of dead-nettle

shaped flowers open from July to September.
Plants may be divided in spring or half ripened wood cuttings rooted in a cold frame in summer.

Arranging

I try to include this little plant in some of my small summer vases because of its unusual flowers which are bright pink with a red and white spotted lower lip. It always adds interest to an arrangement.

Preparation

Lightly hammer stem ends and give a good drink.

Thalictrum

dipterocarpum AGM		1·5 m
dipterocarpum 'Hewitt's Double' AGM		1·2 m
minus adiantifolium		75 cm
speciosissimum (flavum glaucum)		1·5 m

Good deep soil and careful preparation of the site will be repaid with all these species of thalictrum. Each has its own special charm in the herbaceous border.
T. dipterocarpum, with masses of tiny single lilac flowers from July to September and its variety with fully double flowers from June to July, both need careful staking to prevent the weight of blossoms bringing down the stems.
T. minus adiantifolium is an old fashioned cottage garden plant grown chiefly for its maidenhair like foliage.
T. speciosissimum, of larger habit and with handsome grey-green leaves, is perhaps happiest in semi-shade beside an area of bog garden.
T. dipterocarpum is not easy to increase. Plants from seed take three years to reach flowering size.
Mature roots may sometimes be cut in pieces in early spring and with *T. d.* 'Hewitt's Double' if the stems are carefully earthed up, little axillary buds, which may be removed and grown on, will sometimes form in lower leaf axils.
T. m. adiantifolium and *T. speciosissimum* divide readily in early spring.

Arranging

Although the foliage lasts better than the flowers, I still use a few flower stems when in need of some dainty floral material to lighten an arrangement.

Preparation

A diagonal cut and a long drink for the flowers, but give foliage a good drink in deep warm water.

Thuya occidentalis 'Rheingold'

Thuja

occidentalis 'Rheingold' AGM		up to 2 m

Thuja species have pleasantly aromatic foliage and variety 'Rheingold' is a warm, rich golden amber shade, attractive at all times, but specially cheerful in the drab mid-winter months.
It is best treated as a specimen, when the slow growth will be broadly conical. Like the chamaecyparis, basal growths need protection from pets.
The plant needs no regular pruning. Heeled, hard wood cuttings may be taken in autumn and rooted outdoors.
Planting time, as for other evergreens is early autumn or late spring, and the smaller the plant initially, the better the chance of successful transplanting. Larger specimens are however frequently offered and if carefully tended, mulched, watered and sprayed over during dry spells, should transplant without undue difficulty.
Please refer to the chapter on cultural hints for note on special spraying.

Arranging

A beautiful winter foliage which looks best when

arranged with equally bright flowers such as early daffodils.

Preparation
Either hammer or split stem ends and give a good drink.

Tiarella cordifolia (front)

Tiarella

cordifolia	AGM	25 cm
wherryi	AGM	30 cm

Beautiful in both leaf and flower, these little plants in the saxifrage family thrive best in good soil and shady places. They make useful ground cover.

T. cordifolia has bronzy foliage in spring and flowers with dainty heads of small white flowers from May to July.

T. wherryi is a little stouter in habit with prettily

variegated foliage and its flower spikes in creamy white and pink shades appear intermittently from spring until the autumn.

They may be divided after flowering or in early spring. Seed is sometimes available for sowing in a cold frame in spring.

Arranging
The leaves are a real pleasure to use in the base of arrangements and the little creamy white spikes are so pretty in vases of white and green plant material.

Preparation
A diagonal cut and a long drink for the flowers and submerge leaves in cold water for several hours.

A hybrid trollius

Trollius

x *cultorum* 'Alabaster'		50 cm
europaeus 'Superbus'		70 cm
ledebourii 'Golden Queen'		90 cm

The most beautiful of the globe flowers to my mind is still *T. europaeus* but growers are always keen to try new cultivars and this is true too of flower arrangers. Deep, fertile damp soil produces best results with all these trollius. After the spring flowering period, if the plants are happy, odd blossoms will often appear later in the season. The leaves are handsome, shiny and divided, appearing before the flower buds in spring.

Plants may be divided in early spring or after the main flowering period.

Arranging
These yellow globe heads always remind me of kingcups. As they like water I put them in a shallow dish with large leaves at the base and some stones in the water, creating a water garden arrangement.

Preparation
Dip stem ends in boiling water and then give them the deepest drink possible in cold water.

Tropaeolum

majus	2 m
nanum	30 cm
peregrinum	1 – 2 m
polyphyllum	1·5 m
speciosum	2 m

The first three species are annual nasturtiums easily grown from seed sown either indoors in March or outdoors in April. Good soil in sun or shade, against a trellis or along the edge of container, trough or window box is suitable for these plants. The same conditions apply for the dainty canary creeper, *T. peregrinum*.

T. speciosum is perennial, a rather capricious but very beautiful red canary creeper growing from rather fleshy little roots to climb and flower in unexpected places. I have seen it romp through shrubs in a Cheviot farmhouse garden and among evergreens near Loch Lomond. It covers a trellis annually half a mile from my home, but our own little plant rarely reaches 50 cm and never yet has flowered. We keep hoping!

T. polyphyllum is also perennial, though less well known.

Arranging
My first competitive arrangement as a junior flower club member, at the age of eleven, was with nasturtiums in an old conch shell, and I won! So today for sentimental reasons I still arrange them in a shell and they do look effective with their trailing

stems.

Preparation
A diagonal cut and a long drink.

Tulipa kaufmanniana 'Johann Strauss'

Tulipa

greigii	50 cm
kaufmanniana	15 – 40 cm
viridiflora	30 cm

These three tulip species have given rise to lovely varieties now listed in catalogues. All tulips like open sites on beds or for the shorter varieties, on the rock garden. The soil they prefer is light loam and bulbs will increase where soil and climate are suitable – a hot dry summer spell is helpful. On heavier soils it is better to lift the bulbs after foliage has died down and store in dry boxes until November and planting time. 12 cm is amply deep enough for most bulbs. Many of the shorter, early flowering species and varieties grow well in deep pans in cold greenhouse or conservatory.

Arranging

As arrangers, we are so spoiled with the choice of size, shape and colour of the tulips available today that it is difficult to offer advice. The·dwarf varieties mix well with the other spring bulbous material available at the same time. Quite honestly, I feel you can always find a kind of tulip suitable to fit in with any group you may be creating.

Preparation

Cut off the lower, white part of stem, wrap in non-absorbent paper and give a really good drink.

Veronica virginica 'Alba'

Verbascum

bombyciferum	1·2 m
chaixii	60 cm
densiflorum (thapsiforme)	1·2 m

These are easily grown herbaceous plants on any sunny, well drained site and flower over a long period.

V. bombyciferum has large grey felted leaves and is a short lived perennial. However, as seed is freely produced, a stock of these stately plants can be maintained.

V. chaixii also has a grey sheen to its foliage. The flower spikes are branched and each flower has pink stamens. *V. densiflorum* has deep green rosettes of leaves and tall spikes of clustered flowers.

Named varieties from these species can be raised from thick root cuttings in early spring.

Arranging

When in flower these make a nice addition to a mixed summer vase. The silvery leaves are good to use at the base of an arrangement but be careful they do not siphon water out of the bowl. To avoid this remove the fleshy part of the leaf below the water line, leaving only the leaf stem in water.

Preparation

A diagonal cut and a good drink. To dry, remove leaves and hang seed heads upside down.

Veronica

gentianoides 'Variegata'	AGM	45 cm
incana		30 cm
spicata 'Heidikind'		25 cm
teucrium 'Crater Lake Blue'	AGM	30 cm
virginica 'Alba'		1·4 m

These herbaceous species and varieties provide beautiful flowers for the border from May until September. They grow on any good, well drained soil either arranged in small groups or in the case of the dwarf *V. s.* 'Heidikind', along the edge of a border.

V. incana has grey foliage to show off the spikes of deep blue flowers which open from June to August. *V. teucrium* is vivid blue at the same season.

The only white form is a strikingly graceful, late summer species, *V. virginica* 'Alba' which never fails to catch the eye among other border groups.

Veronicas divide readily in early spring or cuttings of young shoots may be rooted in spring.

The shrubby veronicas are now grouped under hebe.

Arranging

The blue varieties provide such a wide range of shades that I always seem to be able to find the appropriate blue for a particular creation. Use them in mixed vases, as the neat spikes give a contrast in shape.

Preparation
Remove lower leaves, make a diagonal cut and give a good drink.

Viburnum

x *bodnantense*	2·5 m
x *burkwoodii* AGM	1·5 m
carlesii AGM	1·3 m
fragrans (farreri) AGM	2 m
x *juddii* AGM	1·3 m
lantana	3 m
opulus 'Sterile' AGM	2·5 m
opulus 'Xanthocarpum' AGM	2 m
plicatum AGM	1·2 m
tinus (laurustinus) AGM	2·5 m
tinus 'Variegatum'	2 m

Most of these species and hybrids are grown for their fragrant heads of white flowers, many of which in the bud stage, are shaded pink. They will grow on most soils and are remarkably hardy, even the winter flowers of *V. fragrans* standing several degrees of frost. *V. lantana* the wayfaring tree grows well on chalky soils and its felty leaves colour richly in autumn. *V. tinus* makes a generous evergreen bush providing both shelter and background for other shrubs, as well as dainty winter blossoms. *V.* x *burkwoodii* is evergreen too but less dense. The leaves are large and shiny. *V. opulus* 'Sterile' is better known as the snowball tree and *V. o.* 'Xanthocarpum' has clear yellow fruits in autumn. Plants may be increased by layering or by half ripened wood cuttings in a cold frame. Berries may be stratified and some species are grafted or budded onto a rootstock.
Little pruning is needed unless *V. tinus* be grown as a hedge.

Arranging
It was difficult to narrow the varieties down to a manageable list as I must confess this is one of my favourites among the shrub genera. I start the year with a few pieces of *V. fragrans* in a specimen vase on my dressing table and then work through the flowering periods of the different species adding stems to mixed arrangements. *V. tinus* is an invaluable asset for providing a year round supply of foliage.

Preparation
Hammer stem ends and dip into boiling water for a few minutes, then give a long drink.

Viburnum tinus

Viburnum plicatum 'Grandiflorum'

The vincas are effective ground coverers

Vitis

coignetiae	AGM	6 – 8 m
vinifera 'Purpurea'	AGM	3 m

These vines are grown mainly for their beautiful coloured autumn foliage. *V. coignetiae* was introduced from the Far East a century ago and has rather rough velvety rounded leaves. It will climb trees and trellises or over pergolas by means of strong tendrils. We have one along the rails of a rustic bridge in company with *Salvia officinalis* 'Tricolor' and *Clematis macropetala*. Little pruning is required. The plant may be increased by hard wood cuttings.

V. v. 'Purpurea' has coloured leaves from spring to autumn, starting red and later turning rich purple. It may be effectively grown through other trees, particularly grey or contrasting leafed species. Should it outgrow the space allocated, prune the side shoots hard back to low buds in late autumn. A check to growth may also be given by stopping the tips of long shoots.

This vine may also be increased by hard wood cuttings.

Arranging

I do not think you can find better leaf material for providing such beautiful autumnal tints. The leaves can be used either individually or in sprays, and can be incorporated with fruit, flowers and berries.

Preparation

Dip stem ends into boiling water for a few minutes then give a long drink. Leaves can be preserved by pressing.

Vinca

major 'Variegata'	AGM	10 cm
minor 'Aureovariegata Alba'		10 cm
minor 'Variegata'		10 cm

The periwinkles are useful evergreen ground cover plants flowering early in the year and continuing throughout the summer. They are happy in sun or shade. The variegated and golden forms are rather less vigorous than the green, but otherwise of similar trailing habit.

It is best to trim over the plants with shears in early spring before new shoots start to grow.

Propagation is easy by division and shoots will often tip-root themselves.

Arranging

What beautiful trails this plant produces, so perfect for cascading from the base of large arrangements.

Preparation

Dip stem ends into boiling water then give a long drink. Spray leaves with a mister.

Vitis coignetiae

Weigela

| florida 'Foliis Purpureis' | 1·3 m |
| florida 'Variegata'   AGM | 1 m |

Useful little deciduous shrubs for town or country gardens on almost any soil, the weigelas have produced interesting small growing variations suitable for gardens with only limited space. The two given here, bear pink flowers in May and June and also have coloured or variegated foliage during spring and summer.

The first has neat purple leaves and the second is green leafed with a creamy white margin.

Both are best pruned straight after flowering. The blooms develop on wood made the previous year and if this flowered wood is cut out, fresh growths will be made in good time for the next year's flowers.

Hard wood cuttings will root fairly easily in autumn.

Arranging

This is a popular summer flowering shrub with arching branches which can be used to produce a flowing line to an arrangement. I also break some of the stems down into quite small sprigs to tuck them into smaller bases. *W. florida* 'Variegata' is particularly attractive.

Preparation

Hammer or split stem ends and give a long drink.

Weigela, a reliable summer flowering deciduous shrub

Zinnia

| 'Envy' | 50 cm |
| 'Lilliput' (miniature pom-pom mixed) | 23 cm |

The gay, half hardy annual zinnias are raised indoors in April for planting outdoors, in warm soil, in late May. They dislike any root check, so prick out early, preferably into small individual pots, but do not sow too soon.

If sown direct on a sunny border in May, thin out the seedlings early. They do not transplant well.

The dwarf varieties in red, gold, lemon and pink shades make very pretty borders. The large green variety 'Envy' has been bred specially with flower arrangers in mind.

Arranging

This genus provides a lovely selection of colours which look best mixed with other summer flowers, as they tend to produce a rather flat effect if arranged on their own.

Preparation

Dip stem ends in boiling water for a minute then give a good drink. Flowers can be preserved in silica gel.

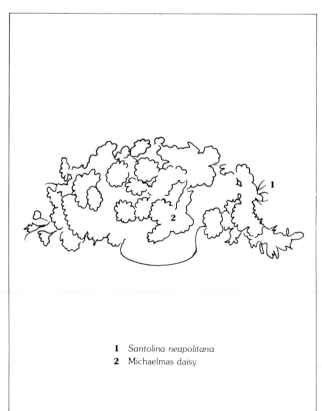

1   *Santolina neapolitana*
2   Michaelmas daisy

ORNAMENTAL VEGETABLES

Cynara

cardunculus 1·5 m
scolymus 'Glauca' 1·8 m

These handsome plants, the cardoon and the globe artichoke respectively, need deep, rich soil and an open site to obtain good foliage and fine flower heads.
To grow new plants, take offsets or suckers from mature plants in April.

Arranging
These plants are a must for large vase arrangements. The silvery foliage makes a striking background for shades of pink and mauve. The giant flowers should be used on short stems as a focal point.

Preparation
Do not cut the foliage too young and when cut, dip stem ends into boiling water and then give a long cold drink. Flower heads just need a long cool drink. Drying of the flower heads takes place naturally on the plant but you can remove the blue scaly part after drying, to reveal a beautiful seed head.

Kale

ornamental 80 cm

A member of the cabbage tribe, seed of this multi-coloured biennial is today included in most seed catalogues for the benefit of the flower arranger. Individual leaves are variegated from autumn until spring or until really hard frost destroys the plants.
Seed is sown in March. Young plants may be set on flower borders, or 60 cm apart along the edge of the brassica bed.

Arranging
Either the leaves or the heart can be used, the heart being placed as a focal point in an all green arrangement while the leaves can be used as part of a mixed group.

Preparation
Cut the heart stem end to a point and then make a cross cut and give a good drink. If using leaves only give their stem ends a diagonal cut.

Cynara cardunculus

Ornamental kale

GRASSES AND SEDGES

Briza media	60 cm
Carex morrowii 'Evergold'	20 cm
Festuca glauca	25 cm
Helictotrichon sempervirens	40 cm
Lagurus ovatus	50 cm
Lasiogrostis splendens	90 cm
Miscanthus sinensis 'Silver Feather'	1·8 m
Molinia 'Moorhexe'	60 cm
Pennisetum orientale	90 cm
Phalaris arundinacea 'Picta'	60 cm
Stipa gigantea	90 cm

Grasses and sedges with decorative foliage and flower heads are becoming more and more widely appreciated for lightening summer borders and for their varied leaf colour in the drab winter months. When starting with seed, mark the site carefully until the seedlings are identifiable from weed grasses. Once established, clumps of perennial species can usually be divided in early spring.

Arranging

The decorative flower spikes of grasses can either be used alone in their fresh state for arrangements of mixed species, or the spikes and leaves may be intermingled with fresh summer flowers. They can also be used dried with other preserved materials for winter vases.

Preparation

Give a long drink. For preserving, pick in full flower just before the pollen anthers appear and glycerine or hang them upside down to dry.

Carex morrowii 'Evergold'

Festuca glauca

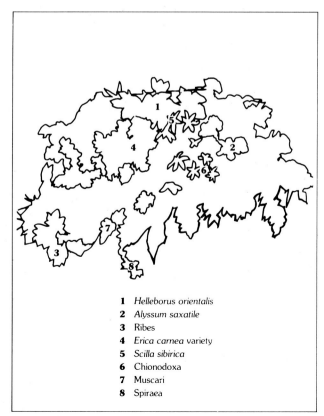

1	*Helleborus orientalis*
2	*Alyssum saxatile*
3	Ribes
4	*Erica carnea* variety
5	*Scilla sibirica*
6	Chionodoxa
7	Muscari
8	Spiraea